Change Agents in High Heels:
7 Influential Women in Coaching REVEAL
How to Transform your
Life, Business, Career, Relationships
(*& almost anything else*)—
With the help of your own Personal Coach

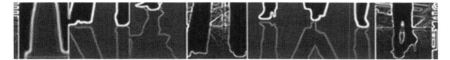

First Class Authors Group
© 2016

Edited by
D. Forbes-Edelen
Jayne Logan

First Class Authors Group
Publishers

Change Agents in High Heels
© 2016. First Class Authors Group
All rights reserved

No claim to copyright is made for original U.S. Government Works.

This book or any portion thereof may not be reproduced or used in any manner whatsoever without the express written permission of the publisher except for the use of brief quotations in a book review and certain other noncommercial uses permitted by copyright law.

For permission requests, write to the publisher, subject line: "Attention: Permissions Authorization," at the following email address: firstclassauthors@gmail.com

Printed in the United States of America

First Printing, 2016

ISBN-13: 978-1523329267

ISBN-10: 1523329262

First Class Authors Group
| A BiziWIFE *Property*

3505 Lake Lynda Drive
Suite 200
Orlando, FL 32825

FirstClassAuthors@gmail.com

Cover Image: Created using Canva.com

Praise for
Change Agents in High Heels

Change is hard. You know that if you've stayed stuck in a bad relationship, unsatisfying career, or unhealthy habit because you're afraid that making a change might make things worse. So like many, you too may decide to stick with the devil you know rather than risk making a change and having to confront a devil you don't know. But when you're finally ready to face these fears and change your life, working with your own Personal Coach may be the answer. If so, then the practical, heartfelt advice given by the 7 Certified Professional Coaches in this book will resonate with you as it has for readers who are saying things like this about **Change Agents in High Heels:**

"A book [that is] a stellar introduction to coaching for the new client." ~Sharon Livingston, Ph D, President ICCA – International Coach Certification Alliance.

"**Change Agents in High Heels** reminded me of why I became a Certified Professional Coach (CPC). Read the book if you're a coach—the reminders will help you remember why you became a coach. Read it if you're thinking of hiring a coach—it's an excellent guide and truly shows the breadth of coaching available.... Where else will you find such a guide on your path to be your absolute best? Find a coach. They help. I know. How? Because I have one (and I am one)." ~Sandra Smart, MBA, CPC. 'The Talent Switch.'

"To share a male perspective on **Change Agents in High Heels**, I loved that the book addressed the need for certification as a qualification for coaches. Although written by 7 different coaches, all of them share a passion for helping people that came through loud and clear, and they got certified to be better prepared do so. A passion to help people is one thing but having the right tools to do so is just as critical. Before reading this book, I had not given much thought about the different types of coaches. Now I appreciate the complexity and diversity of good coaches, as well as what the role of a coach should and should not be. I would not hesitate to pass this on to others."
~Paul Asselin, Retired Manufacturing General Manager. Ottawa, Canada

DISCLAIMER

Although the authors and publisher have made every effort to ensure that the information in this book was correct at press time, the authors and publisher do not assume and hereby disclaim any liability to any party for any loss, damage, or disruption caused by errors or omissions, whether such errors or omissions result from negligence, accident, or any other cause.

DEDICATION

This book is dedicated to all the clients, family, friends, mentors, and fellow coaches we have met along the way.

You are all part of our journey and so remain an indelible part of our story.

We are forever grateful to you all & happy to be so indebted.

TABLE OF CONTENTS

Preface ix

Acknowledgements xi

Introduction xiii

Chapter 1: *So, What Exactly Does a Coach Do?* 1

Chapter 2: *What a Coach is NOT* 14

Chapter 3: *How to Pick the RIGHT Coach* 20

Chapter 4: *How Much Should I Pay for a Coach?* 35

Chapter 5: *What can a Coach Do for YOU?* 41

Chapter 6: *Meet the Coaches* 60

    Renee Asmar 61

    Cynthia Chevrestt 68

    D. Forbes-Edelen 75

    Julie Haggerty 79

    Fran Holinda 90

    Jayne Logan 96

    Jen Ryan 104

Chapter 7: *Final Thoughts* 110

Appendices: *Coaching Resource List* 112

PREFACE

This book began, like most, as an idea.

It became reality because of the dedicated efforts of the contributing authors.

We first met on a cold October morning for advanced professional training. In just a few days we went from strangers to a close-knit, highly supportive team and since then we've become partners and friends.

This book is the result of our search to find a meaningful way to mark the one-year anniversary of our first meeting. It gave us the opportunity to serve the needs of the current and future clients we care so deeply about, while contributing to the advancement of the coaching profession that we hold in such high regard.

Whether you're a coaching client or a coaching professional, we hope this message of service, friendship, and support resonates with you, and, if so, that you will find this book a useful and often used resource for years to come.

ACKNOWLEDGMENTS

This book could not have been written without the help, encouragement, & support of the following people to whom we would like to express our wholehearted thanks and appreciation.

Renee Asmar says an all-inclusive *Thank You* to her family, including her brother Thomas, her confidante and colleague the late Rev. Gerard, along with Denise, Donna and Jim, friends, clients, directees, and sojourners.

Cynthia Chevrestt would like to thank her children Corey & Jada, for all their love and support, especially during the rough times.

Julie Haggerty thanks her loving and supportive husband, children, and grandchildren who fill her life with joy every day.

Fran Holinda would like to thank her fellow *First Class Authors*, a group of amazing ladies who changed her life in 5 days and continue to be her inspiration.

Jen Ryan says a heartfelt *Thank You* to her family and friends who have been so supportive over the years.

Jayne Logan thanks her parents, Roma & Victor, for their support, encouragement, wisdom and, most of all their ever present love and for the incredible life path we all shared. I am *me* because of you.

D. Forbes-Edelen thanks all the family and friends who have been the best part of her life, and Sharon & Glenn Livingston who made this book possible because without them we, the co-authors, would not have met.

INTRODUCTION

This book is the result of the collaborative effort of a group of Certified Professional Coaches who wanted to find a quick, easy, simple, but accurate and balanced resource for educating their clients about what they should and should not expect from working with them—or any other professional coach.

Its goal is to answer the top questions we coaches are constantly being asked by clients and other interested people whose curiosity is peaked, once they learn that we coach people for a living.

Coaching has become the latest buzz word in recent years. It seems that lately everybody is either working with a coach or calling themselves a coach.

People often claim that designation for something as simple as showing someone how to make out a *To Do* list, or for being a shoulder for someone to cry on.

Others call themselves a coach because they have given people personal or professional advice, or shown others how to do a task that falls within their area of expertise.

And, still others call themselves a coach when they are really consultants or mentors.

So, is all just semantics? Are these just different forms of coaching? Is there really any substantive difference between consulting, mentoring, training, support, therapy, or coaching?

The answer is YES!

There is a qualitative difference among these disciplines and coaching. However, this book is not going to focus on providing a side-by-side comparison of the differences among all of these various disciplines (because there are already plenty of other sources that focus on what a consultant, mentor or trainer does). Instead, its focus will be to help you better understand, not only what coaching is and is not—but, how it differs from therapy.

We chose to focus on the difference between coaching and therapy because this is a distinction we feel too few clients and coaches make or make clear enough.

In our view, this blurring of the disciplinary lines do our clients a disservice and can, not only do great harm to them, but to the coaching profession as well.

Besides making this professional distinction clear, this book will answer some of the basic questions that coaches are most often asked by prospective clients and anyone seeking to find their own coach.

So, if you're a current or prospective coaching client, this book has been written to help you better understand what a professional coach does and what this means for you.

If you're a coach, this book will be a useful resource to help you easily and quickly answer most of the common questions you are likely to be asked by those who want to work with you.

Our goal is to help make it easier for fellow coaches to educate their own clients because we believe that educated clients are the BEST clients because they are informed enough to have the best chance to achieve the success they desire—and deserve.

We begin by answering the most common question—and objection—to coaching: *What exactly is coaching and why do I need it?* This is the focus of Chapter 1.

Then we turn our attention to answering other popular questions that we coaches are frequently asked, including:

- *What can coaching do for me that I can't get from going to a therapist or other helping professional?* This is the focus of Chapter 2.
- *How do I pick the Right coach for me?* Chapter 3 answers this question.
- *How much should I pay for a coach?* (See chapter 4).
- *What can I expect a coach to do for ME?* (See chapter 5).

After this you get a chance to meet the contributing coaches and get to know their journeys and how these journeys led them to their chosen coaching specialties (See chapter 6, *Meet the Coaches*).

At the end we provide a short list of *Resources* to help you move forward on your own journey as a coach or coaching client. You'll find these resources in the Appendices.

Finally, a quick note about terminology and the use of personal pronouns.

Throughout this book we use the term, *coach* or *personal coach* to collectively refer to the body of coaching—other than sports or athletic coaching. This can include Life, Health, Business Coaching, or any of the other coaching specialties that exists outside of the sporting arena.

Where the use of the personal pronoun he or she was unavoidable, we deferred to 'she' as a practical necessity, since the co-authors of this book are all females and it helps us to avoid repeatedly using the awkward 'he or she' phrasing. In all instances, though, the use of 'she' is intended to include both men and women.

We hope that you find this book a useful tool and resource for years to come.

Chapter 1

So, Exactly What Does a Coach Do?

*"Life coaching is a **tool** for persons to add to their cache of self-help methods to meet or exceed their personal and professional goals."*—Julie Haggerty

By
D. Forbes-Edelen, Renee Asmar, Cynthia Chevrestt, Julie Haggerty, Fran Holinda, Jayne Logan, Jennifer Ryan

Chapter Introduction
D. Forbes-Edelen

Although *Life Coaching* is not new, if you went to the Bureau of Labor to find out what a professional coach does (outside of the sports arena), you won't find a thing. It is not listed as one of the many occupations recognized by the Bureau.

Yet, if you did a general search on the Internet you'll soon discover that this seemingly invisible occupation—most often known as *Life Coaching*, but also is referred to as, Executive Coaching, Professional Coaching, or Business Coaching—has been recognized as an occupation on the rise for a few decades.

For instance, some sources claim that coaching has been around since the 1980's, as an extension of sports and business coaching.

Others estimate that there are now about 100,000 Certified Professional Coaches (CPC) worldwide who work to assist people to enhance their everyday lives in a wide variety of ways. Whatever statistic you prefer, you will find that there are as many definitions of a non-athletic coach as there are coaching specialists, experts, and coach training organizations.

In any discussion of what a coach does among these experts, you're likely to hear the common themes of accountability, guidance, and facilitating change.

One definition of life coaching that seems to be consistently echoed by many in this profession is the one offered by *Healthcare Career Development* coach, Julie Haggerty, who defines coaching as a self-help *tool* that persons can use to accomplish various goals.

As compelling as this definition is, there *are* other competing ones.

So, rather than impose upon you one or two official definitions of what a coach is, we will go in a different direction.

We'll focus instead on the diversity of views shared by those in the profession, as represented by the co-authors of this chapter.

Since these authors are also practicing coaches, they are in the best position to define what they do.

Let me begin with a personal experience that illustrates my own definition of a coach. It comes from the sports coaching model that most people are familiar with.

> I was in a long-distance race.
>
> After what felt like an eternity, my legs were spaghetti. My sides felt like I was being stabbed from the inside by sharp little needles, and my airways felt like I was sucking air through a straw.
>
> I then saw something in the distance that I thought was the finish line. But, as I got closer, I realized it was a mountain (okay, it was a hill—**Bunker Hill** is the actual name—but it might as well be a mountain because it seemed to fill up the entire earth and looked impassable to me).

Chapter 1: So, Exactly What Does a Coach Do?

It brought me to a standstill; at this point in the race, I decided it was the time to turn back.

But, after a quick assessment of the situation I realized that it was just as far to go back as to go forward; and going back would require just as much pain and effort, so I decided to continue.

Strangely enough, after I made the decision to move forward, that MOUNTAIN seemed much less intimidating.

Eventually I crossed that finish line—or rather, flopped across the line, sort of like an old rag doll. I fell onto the grass and tried to suck up all the air my lungs could hold, while ignoring the persistent pleas of my coach and teammates to, *walk-it-off.*

This was my first experience running a marathon. I did it as part of a High School *Track & Field* Competition.

My High School team was short the few points we needed to win the meet, and the only way we could earn those points was if one of us placed in the top 10 of the final event: a 1 ½ mile mini-marathon.

The problem was that we had no one on our team entered in that event, until my coach asked me to enter.

She chose me, she said, because she was certain that I would finish the race, and that if anyone on the team could finish in the top 10, I was the one.

This experience was a life-defining moment for me, and it illustrates what a coach does (and doesn't do).

My coach knew that I couldn't resist a competitive challenge any more than a bull can resist charging a waving flag.

She knew that if my team needed me, I would do whatever it took to get them the victory. When it mattered most, she knew I would go the distance.

To me, this is the essence of what a coach does—in any field.

As this experience illustrates,

> It's a coach's job to help persons accomplish a prized goal and set them up for success by helping them recognize, access, and actualize their innate strengths, skills, talents and experiences to overcome the mountainous obstacles or *Bunker Hills* that they will encounter along the way to achieving the results that matter to them most—*but it's not a coach's job to do the work for them*—just as it wasn't my coach's job to run the race for me.

So, no matter what your *Bunker Hill* struggle or challenge might be, whether it's how to:

- Make more money
- Make peace with a painful past
- Start or build a lasting relationship with a loving partner
- Win more respect and influence at work or succeed in a career that makes you feel alive
- Feel more beautiful and in control of your life
- Confidently make choices that thrill and fulfill you
- Raise happy, resilient, respectful children—more effortlessly
- Embark on a new business journey
- Make an impact that will define your legacy
- Thrive after a devastating loss, disappointment, or failure

Chapter 1: *So, Exactly What Does a Coach Do?*

It is the job of a personal coach to help you get past your obstacles faster, easier, and with less wasted, time, money, and painful effort.

In the rest of this Chapter, my colleagues describe our job in different ways.

Read on....

The Coach as Facilitator of Change
Fran Holinda

While I do agree with those who describe a coach as an accountability partner and a guide, I would add that the role is much more fluid than that of a mere static partner and guide.

More fundamentally, a coach is a facilitator of transformation.

The coaching process is more than just working to bring about temporary change; it's actually about working toward permanent lifelong transformation.

Coaches must therefore be good communicators and listeners.

Even more importantly, they must be present and adaptable to what their clients need. Accordingly, in any given session, I may be a cheerleader, a guide, a mentor, a motivator, or just a shoulder to cry on.

Yet, while I may wear multiple hats during a coaching session, these changing postures are always guided by a singular focus on honesty and objectivity.

Coaches must be genuine and authentic in order to establish relationships that are built on trust, and they need to have a clear message that resonates with their clients.

My message is, *Change Your Perspective to Change Your Life.*

For me, this means that coaching is not so much about helping people make dramatic changes in their lives; it's more often about helping them to change their perspective about the life they already have.

The Coach as a Resource & Tool

Jen Ryan

Like coach Haggerty, I too fall in the camp of those who see the role of a coach as that of a resource or tool.

In practice, though, the job of a coach is more active than what is suggested by this definition.

For me, this means that, the role of a coach is to actively help individuals break down the barriers that prevent them from being the best version of themselves, so they can maneuver successfully through the stresses of life rather than being overwhelmed by the challenges they're struggling to get past.

In this role,

The coach acts as a mirror to help the client see self-truths and guiding principles that may be self-evident, but are still difficult for them to apply successfully in their lives.

The Coach as Skilled Artisan

Cynthia Chevrestt

Rather than focus solely on what a coach *does*, my definition of a coach tends to focus on the specific skills and qualities that coaches must bring to their job, to be effective.

The most effective coaches must be skilled at asking the right questions, and then they must have the discipline to step back and empower their clients to find their own answers (rather than dictate answers to them).

This point is worth emphasizing.

The importance of allowing clients to find and draw upon the answers within them, and use these answers to create the balanced and fulfilling life they want, cannot be overstated.

As a coach, it's my job to use the right tools and techniques to help clients find these answers within. The most valuable tools I use to do this are my ears.

My first duty is to listen so I can give my clients what they need to take the next step. Only then will I be able to appropriately support and celebrate their successes along the way.

Besides being a perceptive listener, coaches must also be an accountability partner for their clients. In this role, there are clear duties that we owe you, the client. Among these are the duty to,

- **Empower You.** This is your coach's number one duty as an accountability partner. If you're empowered to act on your own behalf, you'll be able to meet and exceed the goals you want to achieve, and you're more likely to live up to your maximum potential—personally and professionally.

- **Help you Explore Options.** It's your coach's duty to be an anchor as you navigate through the sea of options available to you and to be unwavering in their support of you, while you work to figure out the best choices for *you*, based on where you are now, and your vision of where you want to be in the future.

- **Uncover Hidden Blocks.** Your coach owes you his or her keen insight into the blocks that are holding you back from achieving your goals, especially because these blocks are often hidden from you. Once uncovered, your coach has a duty to help you create realistic and practical action steps for getting past these blocks so you can achieve those elusive goals.

- **Create a Safe & Trust-filled Environment.** A coach cannot inspire and empower you to live your own best life without first meeting the duty to make it safe for you to be vulnerable. It is only in a safe and trusting environment that your coach will be able to facilitate your growth.

The Coach as Provocateur

Renee Asmar

Like coach Chevrestt, I agree that the process of asking the right questions and allowing the answers to emerge from the client is indeed an indispensable skill that coaches must bring to the table.

But, to expand on this a bit more, I see this questioning process as not only an interactive and reflective one, but one that is inherently *provocative*—and so the coach's role in this process is that of *provocateur*.

From my perspective, this means that, as provocateur,

> It is the coach's job to instigate and entice the client into animating their strengths and bringing these to bear on the solutions that emerge through the coaching process.

The Coach as an Energy Catalyst

Julie Haggerty

I'd like to underscore and build on this idea of the coach as provocateur, since this is exactly how I too see my job as a coach.

It's important to emphasize that this *provocation* that's instigated by the coach must be done in a non-judgmental environment, if it is to fulfill its potential for transformation.

With this key distinction in mind, I sum up the job of a coach, this way:

> Coaching is an inherently provocative—but non-judgmental—interactive process of questioning, actualizing strengths, and brainstorming client-driven solutions.

This is why I describe the coach's role as that of an, ***energy catalyst.***

As such, the coach's primary job is to motivate and empower clients to activate their own creative powers so they can shift their internal energy from self-doubt to self-belief.

Chapter Summary & Conclusion
Jayne Logan

From my perspective, the story shared by Coach Forbes-Edelen is a wonderful illustration, and encapsulation, of what a coach really is.

She accurately defines our job as working with people to *"set them up for success by helping them recognize, access, and actualize their innate strengths, skills, talents and experiences"* to achieve whatever their goal or definition of success might be.

My own definition of what a coach does is quite simply that a coach is:

> A mentor who helps one to recognize (and bring out) their best *Self,* and then act as a guide and a resource to clients as they travel the path towards accomplishing their goals.

In this chapter, my fellow coaches have provided an excellent overview on what a coach is and the role coaches play in their clients' lives.

We all agree that a coach wears different hats during the coaching relationship. The key is knowing which one is required at any given moment.

So, whether the coach is in the role of an accountability partner and guide; a facilitator of change; an active resource; a skilled listener; or a provocateur, these roles all require the coach to be actively engaged in the process with an inherent belief in the client's potential for success.

Chapter 1: *So, Exactly What Does a Coach Do?*

Now that you have a better idea of what a coach does, it is equally important to know **what a coach is <u>not.</u>**

This is the topic of the next chapter.

Chapter 2

What a Personal Coach is NOT

"A coach does not step inside your inner sanctum boundaries and dictate, advise, or tell you what to do through directives."—Renee Asmar

By

Jennifer Ryan, Cynthia Chevrestt,
Julie Haggerty, D. Forbes-Edelen

Chapter Introduction
Jennifer Ryan

Most people don't understand what a coach is. Some think what we do is a kind of new-age therapy.

To the contrary, coaching is not therapy.

Therapy generally focuses on healing the past. As a coach, it's not my job to help clients fix their past.

True, it is important for me to know my clients' histories, but I focus more on finding a solution to achieve their current goals and help them meet their positive future self.

This moving forward towards positive future change is the job that clients hire coaches to do.

In this chapter we focus on the distinction that all coaches (and their clients) must make, between coaching and therapy.

A Personal Coach is NOT a FIXER nor FRIEND

Cynthia Chevrestt

A coach is **NOT** your therapist or your friend. A coach does not fix your problems.

A good coach will hold you accountable for taking practical actions to solve your problems, and such a coach will challenge you to grow and do more than you think you can do, which may be uncomfortable at times.

Your coach should thus help you stretch beyond your comfort zone and encourage you to let go of some of the behaviors and ways of thinking that no longer serve you.

This means that your coach may not always tell you what you want to hear—but will tell you what you need to hear in order to make positive and effective changes in your life so you can move forward and fulfill your goals and dreams.

Clearly, if you're not capable of actively taking charge of your own transformation—for whatever reason—a coach will not serve you well.

A professional coach will tell you this honestly—but tactfully.

The Coach is NOT Focused on the Past
Julie Haggerty

While coaches never act in the capacity of a therapist (even if they are trained mental health professionals), they must still be able to distinguish between the mentally ill and the mentally healthy.

Like many other coaches, I draw the line between coaching and therapy based on whether or not the problem the client wants to solve is focused on issues of the past or future.

A past-orientation falls within the domain of the therapist, while a future-orientation is the exclusive domain of the coach.

In other words, a coach's playing field is the future.

This is the domain that coaching alone occupies and that coaches are trained to act upon, on their clients' behalf.

Unlike a therapist, therefore, a coach is duty-bound to effect positive changes in the client's future. To do so they must maintain a singular and unwavering focus on where the client wants to go, rather than where the client has been.

Chapter Summary & Conclusion
D. Forbes-Edelen

As demonstrated by the coaches in this chapter, there is virtually universal agreement among professional coaches that,

Coaches are <u>NOT</u> Therapists.

Where their views diverge is *how* they make this distinction between coaching and therapy.

For many, the difference between the two disciplines is the operating assumption that guides their interventions.

The operating assumption of a therapist or mental health practitioner is that the client is *sick* and needs to be healed.

By contrast, the operating assumption of a coach is that their clients are *healthy* but blocked by a formidable challenge that they need help to push past.

Nevertheless, in her Harvard Business Review article, Diane Kauffman cites researchers at the University of Sydney who found that, "25 to 50 percent of coaching clients reported clinically significant levels of anxiety, stress, or depression."

Given this research finding, the reality is that coaches are highly likely to encounter persons with mental illnesses, whether or not they are so diagnosed.

Accordingly, they must be prepared to recognize the signs of undiagnosed (or not obvious) mental health problems in clients who seek them out and then be ready to handle these cases appropriately.

This is one reason why I recommend working with a Certified Professional Coach (CPC).

A coach with this professional designation will have received specialized training and supervised practice in directing the mentally ill to appropriate resources to get the help they really need.

As the certified coaches in this chapter have shown, they meet the challenge of distinguishing between the mentally sick and mentally healthy in two basic ways *(besides, of course, suicidal ideation, which is a clear sign of mental illness that all professional coaches recognize).*

These two criteria are:

- If the problem the client wants to solve is focused on issues of the past or future. Clients whose problems are focused on the past are likely to be referred to mental health professionals.

- The locus of control that solving the client's problem demands. Since coaches agree that the locus of control must remain with the client, if control over the solution shifts from the client to the professional, then the relationship has crossed the line from coaching to therapy and a mental health referral may be appropriate.

I use both of these criteria, in addition to cognitive functioning.

I will also consider whether a client's judgment seems so impaired by a lack of self-insight and self-awareness that this one is unable or unwilling to function socially or follow through on basic self-care, like eating, bathing, and grooming, etc.

However, once such individuals regain their mental health, I am willing to work with them on specific goals that they are now healthy enough to attain.

In rare instances, I will work with mentally ill clients in close cooperation with their therapist.

Chapter 2: *What a Personal Coach is NOT*

If you're curious about what it looks like when a coach and therapist works together, here's an example of how this might work:

> A client, who we'll call *Suzy*, may be seeing a therapist to understand why she's unable to break free from certain negative thinking. Thus, the therapeutic goal of her therapist would be to help her figure out the source of her negative thinking patterns and how past experiences trigger such thinking in her life now.
>
> Accordingly, the therapist's interventions would focus more on figuring out the cause of the problem—in the hopes that understanding the source of the problem behavior will be enough to help *Suzy* put a stop to it.
>
> By contrast, *Suzy's* coach would work with her to put together a practical, focused, plan of action for breaking free of one or more specific negative thinking patterns.
>
> Although her coach might have some interest in knowing what may have caused the problem in the first place, *Suzy's* coach still cares less about the original cause or source of her problem—and more about helping *Suzy* to put a stop to it.

Notwithstanding these rare instances when a coach might work with a therapist, the main point we want to make in this chapter is that coaches are <u>not</u> therapists, so before you hire your own personal coach, take the time to first find out this coach's policy on working with and referring mentally ill clients.

Now that you know what a coach *does* and *does not* do, the next obvious question is: ***How do you choose the right one for <u>you</u>?***

This question is the focus of the next chapter.

Chapter 3

How to Pick the RIGHT Coach for YOU!

"The qualities the client brings to the relationship are paramount to achieving successful coaching results."—Renee Asmar

By
Renee Asmar, Jennifer Ryan, Jayne Logan,
Cynthia Chevrestt, D. Forbes-Edelen

Chapter Introduction
Renee Asmar & Jennifer Ryan

As the opening quote suggests, the qualities that clients bring to the relationship are paramount to achieving successful coaching results.

These client qualities include:
- Honesty
- Accountability
- Being fully invested
- A willingness to tolerate the discomfort of being stretched and challenged
- A willingness to step outside their comfort zone to achieve their desired results.

The importance of the client's role in achieving good coaching outcomes suggests that selecting the right coach is more of an intuitive process than a prescriptive one, in which a person follows a set of prescribed rules.

Chapter 3: *How to Pick the RIGHT Coach for YOU!*

So, the key to finding a coach that's right for you is to ask a lot of questions. A good place to start is to ask for recommendations from among your network of friends and acquaintances.

Then,

If the answers to your questions raise any *red flags* that make you feel you cannot trust the coach you're considering working with, then walk away and find another coach (even if you cannot quite *put your finger* on why you question this coach's trust).

In the rest of this chapter, coaches Logan, Chevrestt, and Forbes-Edelen provide other important criteria to use in selecting the right coach for YOU.

In Selecting the RIGHT Coach, Context Matters

Jayne Logan

The interactivity of coach and client is vital to achieving successful coaching outcomes. Therefore, the context each party contributes to the coaching process is crucial.

It is important that both clients and coaches understand there is no such thing as a one-size-fits-all approach.

Each person comes to their coach with a different frame of reference formed through life experiences, cultural influences, and a myriad of circumstances.

So, while there may be similarities between the goals of different clients, every individual is truly unique and the coaching approach should be the same.

Given the importance of personal context, selecting the right coach must start with a genuine interpersonal connection.

If you are unable to relate to each other you'll probably find that you'll accomplish very little with this coach, which is no fun for either party.

It can end in frustration and lost time and opportunity for the client, and in lost credibility for the coach.

This is why the initial consultation is so invaluable.

It gives both parties an opportunity to create a positive starting point for establishing an environment of trust.

In this context-driven process, the other significant factor for success is a willing client.

Chapter 3: *How to Pick the RIGHT Coach for YOU!*

By willing, I mean the client must be highly motivated to change and ready to do the necessary work.

And, make no mistake, there <u>IS</u> work involved.

Contrary to what some may believe, coaching is far from easy, although it <u>IS</u> rewarding. So, there has to be firm commitment and buy-in on both sides.

Certainly, the coach is the facilitator whose job it is to bring about lasting and meaningful change, but all of the heavy lifting (or the real work) is done by the client.

Considering the importance of context and shared-responsibility in the coaching relationship, the philosophy that guides a coach's methods and decisions is important.

That's why I recommend that you select a coach who can articulate a clear set of guiding principles that underlie the methods that she will use in working with you.

If the coach you're thinking of hiring cannot do this, the chances for success diminishes, thus it may be in your best interest to look for someone else.

My coaching philosophy is fairly simple. I have a strong belief that,

> *There is <u>always</u> a way, IF you are committed.*

This is the underlying principle that guides my approach, the questions I ask, the methods I use, and the actions I ask clients to take.

For example, some clients come to the coaching relationship with fear and skepticism; they fear the commitment and are skeptical of their ability to succeed because their past efforts did not create the results they wanted.

Based on my philosophy that **commitment creates the way**—when a client says,

> *"Nothing I've tried has ever worked"*

I ask them to consider finishing their statement by adding, **"Up until now."**

It's a true statement for them, and one they can believe.

Furthermore, it validates what they've stated.

I offer no judgment on what they've tried in the past, or why things didn't work.

This gives them permission to start anew and put the past behind them, thus creating space for the idea that they CAN successfully make a change.

This simple approach (informed by my coaching philosophy), can put clients on a path that will enable them to see a light at the end of the tunnel of self-doubt, and begin to believe in themselves and the possibilities available to them.

So, how do you find a coach with these important qualities?

> *Do your research!*

Start by asking questions like those I've placed in Appendix 1 at the end of this book, and do a test-drive before you commit to a longer relationship.

This is one of the main reasons I offer (and in fact insist upon), a one-hour complementary session before I even agree to work with a client.

Chapter 3: *How to Pick the RIGHT Coach for YOU!*

This gives prospective clients an opportunity to ask as many questions as they would like and it allows me to make sure they understand exactly who I am, and what they are getting into.

Some of the questions you should consider when interviewing a prospective coach are:

- What is your coaching philosophy?
- Do you have a formal coaching agreement? Does it outline the responsibilities of both coach and client? Does it explain your terms, confidentiality, and other policies?
- Why did you choose to become a coach?
- Are you certified? By Whom?

The answers to these questions will help you decide if a prospective coach has a philosophy that you are drawn to, and will allow you to validate this person's credentials for yourself.

The information you glean will also help you determine whether the coach has a framework for the coaching relationship that consists of clear Rules of Engagement, which should be clearly specified in a written **Coaching Agreement.**

Having the rules and expectations written down like this ensures there are no unhappy surprises, and it will set the right tone of professionalism—one that indicates you are both serious and committed to doing the work required.

Finally, in view of the contextual nature of the coaching process, what you learn during your research should give you a very good sense of the qualities and background that this particular coach brings to the relationship.

Knowing this will give you a better feel for whether or not this coach is objective, open-minded, non-judgmental, and focused on your best interests—not their own.

In particular, pay attention to the prospective coach's story.

Learning why someone chose to become a coach will give you a real flavor for who they are, and whether or not you will be able to relate well to them.

No matter who you eventually choose to work with, it's important to remember this caution:

> A coach does not have all the answers—but she should be an expert at asking the right questions.

So do not expect your coach to be able to tell you what to do.

A coach who does this has crossed the ethical boundaries and is one you should be wary of.

Chapter 3: *How to Pick the RIGHT Coach for YOU!*

Choosing the RIGHT Coach Starts with Knowing the Costs of NOT Hiring a Coach

Cynthia Chevrestt

When it comes to choosing the right coach, you have to begin with absolute clarity about your needs, wants, expectations, and, most importantly—the costs of **NOT** hiring the right coach.

This clarity is important because the more clear and specific you are about what you want to achieve, the better your chances of finding the right coach to get you there.

Yet, just as important (if not more so), is also understanding the costs of **NOT** hiring a coach.

I learned this lesson the hard way.

My own personal experience taught me that *not* having a coach to hold me accountable was far more expensive, time consuming, and draining on my mind, body, and soul than any amount of time and money I could've ever invested in working with one.

Most of my life I've done everything on my own because I used to feel that asking for help was a form of weakness.

Now I know better.

The truth is, asking for help and being open and coachable is actually a great strength; in fact, *not* asking for help is the real sign of weakness.

Although you can certainly accomplish many things on your own, having someone in your corner to coach, guide, and hold you accountable sets you up for success and is a quicker, safer, and a lot less expensive way to achieve your dreams.

So, once you're ready to get the help you need, one of the best ways to select the best coach for you is to choose one who has gone through what you're going through and survived it and can now help you do the same.

This will be the ideal coach for you because this is someone who will have the tested tools and insights you will need to get past the pitfalls, roadblocks, and ups and downs you're going to encounter on the way to achieving your own goals.

I'm often asked if certification is the best (or even if it's a necessary) indicator of a good coach.

When it comes to the question of certification, just as there is no, one-size-fits-all coaching method, there are also no one-sized-fits-all certification criteria.

Therefore, the thing to remember about the difference between a certified and uncertified coach is that a certified coach has received training in specific tools, skills, and techniques to help you most efficiently; an uncertified coach is less likely to have developed such a proven and varied skill-set.

So, if it's important to you to work with a coach who has a tested toolbox of coaching methods and techniques—and the proven skills to use them properly—then you should definitely choose a Certified Professional Coach (CPC).

Nevertheless, whether you work with a certified coach or not, the bottom line is that each individual is different and so is each coach.

Given this reality, one low-risk way to make sure that you choose a coach that's a good fit for you is to request a FREE *Getting to know you Session,* before making your decision.

Doing this will give you a sense for whether or not there's a connection between you and the coach you're thinking of hiring.

Chapter 3: *How to Pick the RIGHT Coach for YOU!*

At the end of the day, the thing that really drives the best coaches is the personal fulfillment we get when our clients feel empowered or when they achieve their ultimate goals or when they tell us how much happier and more purposeful their lives have become.

If these are the ways you want to feel about your own life, then spend whatever time it takes to find and work with the right coach.

It is an investment that can produce priceless rewards, far beyond the financial cost.

I know. I've done it.

I am living proof of the priceless benefits of working with the right coach, at the right time.

Chapter Summary & Conclusion
D. Forbes-Edelen

In closing out this chapter, I'll like to expand on the discussion of certification as a criterion in selecting the right coach.

As the discussions in this chapter suggest, choosing the right coach can be daunting, especially since there currently are no 'official' credentialing requirements or other universal industry standards to use as a guide.

Frankly, this means that anyone can hang a sign, say they are a coach, and start doing business.

In response to this wild-west environment, some have established certification programs to promote professionalism in the industry. This is a promising sign.

How important then is certification? The short answer is, *it depends.*

While it can be prudent to look for a coach who has taken the time and expense to get certified, since this demonstrates a commitment to professional growth and skills development, not all certifications are created equally.

Thus, the quality of your coach's certification program merits close scrutiny. So take the time to find out where your coach received his or her training and certification. Check to see how it measures up to the following key indicators of a high quality training and certification program:

- **The Board of Directors.** Who are the members of the board and what are their credentials, experience, and training?

Chapter 3: *How to Pick the RIGHT Coach for YOU!*

- **The Curriculum.** How many hours of coaching practice is required for certification? Anything less than 24 hours of coaching practice, under the supervision of qualified Master Coaches is questionable. Similarly, there should be a variety of techniques, theories, and methodologies included in the program. If the coach has been certified by a one-sized fits all type of curriculum, be cautious.

- **Duration of the program.** If the program is a *Get Certified in 72-hours* kind of program, this should raise a red flag. Coaching is a people skill. It demands that a new coach spend time in front of people to become skilled enough to be entrusted with your money, time, and trust.

- **Professional Development Requirement.** Is ongoing professional development and training provided or offered or encouraged? If not, it may be time to seek out a different coach whose certification is from a more rigorous coaching program.

- **Code of Ethics.** Does it clearly distinguish between coaching and therapy? Does it require its certified coaches to follow a clearly articulated *Code of Ethics* that hold them accountable for crossing the line between the two or harming their clients in any other way?

Admittedly, though, even if a coach graduates from the best certification program, this does not necessarily mean this one is the best coach for *you*.

Besides certification, there are a few other common-sense criteria to look for, as discussed in this chapter.

As the coaches repeatedly advised, the ability to listen perceptively is the one essential skill to look for in selecting your coach.

Listening is critically important because a coach has to be able to ask you the right questions; this is impossible for a coach to do without first listening to you on a deep and intimate level.

Coaches must also have the self-discipline to get out of your way and allow you to discover the right answers for *you*—without imposing their own answers on you.

Given the dual importance of a coach's ability to listen astutely and probe unobtrusively, it should be self-evident that these are skills that take time to develop.

This is why looking for a coach with many hours of proven professional experience, is a good start; but it's not enough.

To ensure that you get the best possible outcomes and results, you must also work with a coach who is a good fit for you.

Of course, evaluating what makes someone a *good fit* is a subjective process—one that should begin with identifying a coach whose specialty is in the specific area you're struggling with, rather than a generalist.

In other words, rather than hiring a general life-coach, hire a coach who specializes in the type of transformation you want to achieve—the more specific, the better.

For example, if you want to lose 50 pounds before your wedding in six months, hiring coach who specializes in safe and rapid weight-loss strategies will serve you better than hiring a general health, fitness, or life coach.

The bottom-line is that you're more likely to get the best outcomes if you hire a coach who can clearly tell you what will change for you after working with him or her.

A coach who cannot or will not do this, may not have a well thought out process or structure for helping you and will

Chapter 3: *How to Pick the RIGHT Coach for YOU!*

probably be *winging* it, which means that, at best, you'll be paying for hit or miss results.

If the best that a coach can offer you is an occasional accidental success—what good is that result to you and why would you want to pay good money for results you could've stumbled onto by yourself—*for FREE?*

You deserve more than this for your time and money.

Here then are three commonsense questions to consider when evaluating a coach you're thinking of hiring:

- **How well-aligned are your values?** For example, if your coach is guided by spiritual values that are contrary to your own, you may find the relationship constraining and stifling.

- **How well do your personalities mesh?** If your coach is a tell-it-like-it-is or tough-love kind of coach, but you respond better to a more empathetic, lift you up kind of approach, you may find the coaching relationship bruising to your self-esteem.

- **What is the coach's Coaching Philosophy?** If your coach's philosophy emphasizes methods that involve guided meditation but such techniques make you break out in a cold sweat—you're going to probably find the coaching relationship limiting, stressful, and self-defeating.

Hopefully, you now have a good idea of how to select the best coach for you and what role certification should play in your final decision.

Now that you know what criteria to use in selecting your coach, you're probably thinking about another common question about coaching:

How much do coaches charge?

The next chapter answers this question.

Chapter 4

How Much Should I Pay for a Coach?

*"The answer to the question of how much should I pay for a coach depends on the **value** individuals place on achieving their goals."*— Julie Haggerty

By

Julie Haggerty & D. Forbes-Edelen

Chapter Introduction
Julie Haggerty

Actually, instead of asking, *how much should a coach cost?*

The more useful question to consider in hiring a coach is this: *Is the investment is worth the desired outcome?*

Since people are more apt to work harder to be successful if they are held accountable, hiring a certified professional can be the coaching equivalent of investing in your own personal *CliffsNotes* for life.

Just as you might purchase *CliffsNotes* for a course to shorten the learning curve that can make learning a new subject longer and more arduous than it needs to be, coaches can do the same thing for you by shortening the distance from **Dreams to Plans to Goals Accomplished.**

If this shortcut is valuable enough to you, then you should be willing to pay the price to get the best qualified help available.

In this chapter,

Coach Forbes-Edelen summarizes the key factors that we all agree will help you to figure out how to measure the value of coaching to you so you can better determine the right investment you need to make to get this value.

Summary & Conclusion

If You Want to Pay Peanuts, You May Wind Up Hiring Monkeys for a Coach

D. Forbes-Edelen

As coach Haggerty correctly points out, the value of the desired outcome is an important factor in determining the price you will pay for coaching.

Various industry surveys put the median fee in the range of $200 to $500 per hour, depending on the areas of specialty and other qualifications, such as certification.

Generally, business and certified professional coaches command the highest fees compared to life-coaches who typically (but certainly, not always) tend to be found at the lower end of the fee spectrum.

For example, in the current market, Harvard Business Review puts the fees for corporate-level executive coaches around $3500 per hour, while other coaching authorities put the fees for personal development and life coaching specialties in the $100 to $300 per hour range.

Our advice is that price alone is *NEVER* an adequate measure of the quality of a coach, so do not be tempted to go for the cheapest person you can find (or the most expensive, for that matter) because frankly,

> *If you insist on paying peanuts,*
> *you may end up hiring monkeys for a coach*

Hence, it's worth repeating that, if the goal or result you want to achieve matters to you, it's worth spending the money that the transformation you're looking for requires (no more, no less).

In the long run this approach will save you money and get you where you want to go in the shortest possible time and with the least amount of pain.

The good news is that many coaches are willing and able to structure their fees to fit your needs by adjusting the number or frequency of your sessions together. So, before you conclude that a coach you really want to work with is financially out of reach for you, it's always a good idea to ask the coach if this option is available.

In addition to the result you want to achieve, some of the other factors that will determine the fee you're likely to pay are (1) experience, (2) the level of customization, and (3) the time-frame anticipated for achieving results.

Obviously, you will pay more for experienced coaches, especially if they are also certified.

You will also pay more for individualized coaching because it is much more customized compared to a group program, in which there is less customization and the costs are spread among several people.

Additionally, if a coaching program is customized in any unique way (whether for individual needs or based on group preferences)—the investment will also land on the higher end of the fee spectrum.

Similarly, the longer the coaching relationship lasts, the higher the financial investment will be. But, it is equally true that if quick results in a short time-span is the goal, you will pay a premium.

Chapter 4: *How Much Should I Pay for a Coach?*

Generally, you should expect to work with a coach for at least 30-days to get the most fruitful and sustainable results.

On average, coaches report working with clients for about 6-12 months, with some relationships lasting a year or more. The general industry consensus is that 90-days or longer is the norm.

Besides, experience, customization, and the time-frame involved, another factor that will determine the price you pay is the pricing model being used.

An emerging trend is the pay-for-results fee model.

This is where the client pays for specific results rather than by the hour, similar to the way sports coaches are paid.

You probably know that sports coaches are hired to achieve a specific goal, such as helping a sports team or athlete win a prized championship or make the Olympic team or get in peak condition for a high-stakes competition.

Similarly, coaches who follow the pay-for-results fee model will charge a specific fee to achieve a clearly defined, usually, high-stakes goal.

For instance, a business or marketing coach might be paid a specific fee to help clients increase sales and conversion rates or reduce losses, by a certain percentage or attract a highly desirable VIP client.

Or, a team building coach might be paid specifically to improve customer retention or team effectiveness on a high-budget project.

While this results-driven fee model is currently used most often in the business coaching arena, it is increasingly being adopted across other coaching specialties, in place of the standard cost-per-hour pricing model.

Now that you've decided to pay for your own coach, it may be helpful to know the answer to the question,

What can working with a coach do for me?

This is the subject of the next chapter. Each of the contributing-authors and coaches discuss what they actually **do** for the people who come to them for help.

The transformations these coaches help their clients to achieve will give you good insight into what you can expect to achieve with the help of your own personal coach.

Chapter 5

What Can a Personal Coach Do for <u>YOU</u>?

"Coaching is an intangible; and, even with testimonials, there are no before and after transformation photos to browse through so people can easily see what a coach can do for them." —Fran Holinda

By
Julie Haggerty, Jayne Logan, Fran Holinda, Jen Ryan, Cynthia Chevrestt, Renee Asmar, D. Forbes-Edelen

Chapter Introduction
Julie Haggerty

So, what can a coach do for <u>YOU</u>?

Well, if you think of coaching as a verb, you'll see that it's not just some abstract event; it is an action.

It requires that the person being coached actually *do* something, and be held accountable for doing it.

If you are reading this book you've probably wondered, at some point, what a life coach can actually help you accomplish.

Below is a short list of a few of the problems that coaches in different areas of specialty can help you solve.

Short List of Selected Problems Coaches Help to Solve

Weight Loss	Learn to develop strategies to achieve goals	Vocational achievement
Personal Growth	How to achieve life enjoyment	Writing achievement
Becoming unstuck or *"rut busting"*	Life mapping	Mapping out the perfect gardening plan to feed your family
Work/home life balance	Life transitioning	Career pathways
Breaking negative thinking patterns or *black and white thinking*	Strengthening personal relationships	Home/work organization
Strategies to live a happy minimalist life	Health and Fitness strategies to live a strong, healthy life	Crisis management strategies

Source: Julie Haggerty| ©2016

In the rest of this chapter, the coaches discuss what they have been able to do for their clients and the approaches they use to achieve these results.

Their discussions demonstrate the type of results you can expect from working with your own coach and will give you insight into how a coach's journey can influence her choice of specialty and preferred coaching methods.

Chapter 5: *What Can a Personal Coach Do for <u>YOU</u>?*

So here's your coaching assignment:

> As you read through these coaches' personal stories, think about what they reveal about what working with your own personal coach can do for *you*.
>
> Then, I challenge you to pick up the phone, log onto a computer, go to a library, check out your local community center, or ask your family, friends, and colleagues for a recommendation, and schedule a FREE 30-minute consultation with a prospective coach.

A thirty-minute conversation, with the right one, is all it should take to convince you of the *value* of having the right coach in your corner.

> Ding, Ding, Ding! Get going. Your time starts NOW!

I'd love to hear how you're doing with this challenge. Let me know what you discover.

A Coach Can Help YOU

Challenge the Status Quo & Break Free of Self-Imposed 'Rules' that No Longer Serve You Well

Coach Jayne Logan

One of my favorite quotes by Sir Winston Churchill captures what I feel a coach can do for anyone.

> *"Every day you may make progress. Every step may be fruitful. Yet there will stretch out before you an ever-lengthening, ever-ascending, ever-improving path. You know you will never get to the end of the journey. But this, so far from discouraging, only adds to the joy and glory of the climb."*

The point of this quote is that, life is a journey where there'll be twists and turns and peaks and valleys, but the real joy comes from living the best story you can create.

While the reasons that people seek a coach varies widely, these reasons can be boiled down to one thing: *a desire for change.*

However, not everyone comes to a coach with a specific destination in mind. Consistent with the old axiom that people will do more to avoid pain than to gain pleasure, many seek out a coach after they've tried everything, but nothing has worked and their current situation has become so painful that remaining static feels much riskier than taking action.

Others seek out a coach after observing its positive effects in the life of a friend, co-worker, or family member and they too want to experience similar results.

Chapter 5: What Can a Personal Coach Do for *YOU*?

However, whether motivated by internal forces such as the emotional turmoil of struggling to reach an elusive goal or by external pressures related to their career or any other areas of life, there is a coach for every situation.

Still, it is important to keep in mind that there are no quick fixes.

Your results are often a question of timing and your willingness to do the necessary work.

When the real or potential consequences of your current situation becomes so painful that your desire to remove the pain outweighs your resistance to doing the work required to make meaningful and lasting change, this is when working with your own coach will produce the best and fastest results.

I mentioned earlier that one way to get a feel for who is the right coach for you is to understand their story. Well, similarly, knowing why someone chose to become a coach is also a good way to tell what a prospective coach can do for you.

My own personal journey appears in the next chapter and reveals a lot about what people can expect from working with me.

If what it reveals about my coaching style resonates with you, feel free to reach out to me. I'd love to meet you!

A Coach Can Help YOU

Shift Your Perspective on Beauty, Aging, & the Rewards of Living Life from the 'Inside-Out'

Coach Fran Holinda

Coaching isn't always about helping people achieve something specific or make a dramatic change in their lives.

As my own journey demonstrates, many times it's about helping them to find contentment and happiness with the life they already have.

My journey began in the fitness industry.

In the fitness world, I saw so many people who were willing to spend ridiculous amounts of money on diet, exercise, food and more—primarily to improve their outside appearance (even if they wanted health benefits, as well).

These people would spend hours looking at before and after pictures of bodies that had been beautifully transformed after working with one personal trainer or another.

They believed that getting physically fit would instantly make them fabulous, so they didn't need to be convinced of the benefits of getting in shape.

By contrast, it is so much more difficult to convince people that they also need to work on their inner beauty—which I believe is actually more important—but not as visible a result as a beautiful body.

Chapter 5: What Can a Personal Coach Do for *YOU*?

This is why, as I said in my opening quote, it can be hard for coaches to convince people of the value of their work, since the transformations that coaching produce are largely intangible.

Thus, even with testimonials, there are still no before and after photos for people to browse through to see what inside fitness and beauty might look like for them. So, it's not as easy for people to convince themselves that it's worth the effort to work with a life coach.

Admittedly, convincing people of the intangible benefits of personal coaching has made my own coaching journey frustrating at times, but as you will see when you read my story in the next chapter, it has also been quite rewarding.

The rewards have come from having had the privilege of working with clients who understand the benefits of working on their inner beauty as the first important step to achieving their goals. It is truly a high to know you've played such a pivotal role in someone's life.

This is the kind of impact I've wanted to make all my life. I guess that's why I've wanted to be a teacher since I was 5 years old.

I would practice making stars on paper with crayons while pretending I was grading student papers.

So, I suppose, for me, coaching is a form of teaching.

But, instead of talking at students and telling them what they need to know, I talk *with* clients and help them to discover what they already know.

If you'd like to work on making some inside discoveries together, reach out to me. I'm always eager to hear from you.

A Coach Can Help YOU

**Achieve Professional & Personal Life Balance
So You Can Perform at Your Peak at Home, Work & Business**

Coach Jen Ryan

My coaching philosophy can be summed up as follows:

> *"Discovering your unique talents allow
> You to achieve your ultimate goals."*

It was developed after almost 25 years of coaching and mentoring people in a variety of circumstances.

Through this experience, I discovered that my greatest strengths are my intently focused listening skills and my ability to stay present.

These talents give me unique insights to a person's *why*—which is the key to moving forward in a positive direction.

When people are clear on their own *why* it helps them figure out what they really want. This clarity is so important that, helping clients figure out their *why* is where my own work with them begins.

I especially enjoy it when the women I work with have that one moment when they reach a goal or milestone without realizing it because they are so busy on their journey that it just happens naturally.

Chapter 5: What Can a Personal Coach Do for <u>YOU</u>?

In the past, I've worked with professionals, business owners, and staff-level employees to solve productivity and customer service problems. While I still enjoy that role, I now primarily work with successful career women on work-life balance issues.

As you will see when you read my story in the next chapter, I feel it is an honor, rather than just a job, to be able to help people be successful at being the best version of themselves.

For me, true joy comes from doing what I love and making a living at it, which is something relatively few people ever succeed at doing because they are too busy being successful at the wrong things.

Success at the wrong things—even if you're good at it—is a recipe for unhappiness.

Yet, most of the people I've worked with over the years are often surprised to discover that this is why success hasn't always equaled happiness for them.

This is why my top goal when working with clients is to help them find the best version of themselves and live it successfully.

For many, this can be very difficult to do because of their self-limiting beliefs and lack of support.

Hence, these are the two biggest problems I help my clients to solve.

I help them conquer their self-limiting beliefs by looking at things in new ways. Along with this, I provide the support they need to become more confident and fearless in confronting the challenges and obstacles they encounter along the way.

I look forward to challenging your assumptions and to supporting you on your journey.

If my story and coaching philosophy feels like a good fit, let me know.

I would love to hear your story, and I'd like to give you the tools you need to bring the balance into your life that you need to always perform at *your* peak!

Chapter 5: What Can a Personal Coach Do for YOU?

A Coach Can Help YOU
Aim Higher, Achieve More, & Rebuild a GREAT Life After Deep Despair, Disappointment, or Guilt

Coach Cynthia Chevrestt

This quote from Michelangelo is one of my favorites:

> *"The greater danger for most of us is not that our aim is too high and we miss it, but that it is too low and we reach it."*

I love it because it really sums up what I do for my clients:

I help them to aim higher—and reach it.

People will work with personal coaches like me when they want to feel happier, get paid well doing what they love to do, and finally start living the life they dream about.

If this sounds like you, then you've probably tried many other solutions by now.

You may have tried reading self-help books, seeing a therapist, or talking with a spiritual advisor or others in the helping professions, or you may simply have sought advice from family and friends.

If any of these worked for you, great! Keep doing what you're doing.

But if you're still struggling to get what you want after trying to do it all on your own, then working with a personal coach can be the answer, especially if you're not sure what you want or where you want to go, or how to figure this all out.

And, even if you *do* know what you want, a coach can still help you—if you're struggling to figure out what steps to take to get it.

The reason that I'm so confident that a personal coach can help you is because of my own experience.

As you will learn when you read my story, I discovered who I wanted to serve as a coach after going through an intense, but transformative, emotional breakdown.

It happened out of the blue one morning when I was suddenly flooded with past memories of the struggles and guilt I had endured when I had to leave my young children for long deployments.

The tears I cried that morning released over a decade of bottled up stress, guilt, and despair that I had been too embarrassed to share with anyone as I tried to handle it all alone.

It didn't work.

However, after my breakdown, things changed. The self-discoveries that I made afterwards were like an awakening.

They forced me to ask for help—not from mental health professionals, as you might expect—but from my own personal coach.

With the help of my coach, I was able to turn this breakdown into a breakthrough, and this is what I try to help other women to do, especially those who like me, are veterans and single-mothers.

Chapter 5: What Can a Personal Coach Do for YOU?

Like me, these women veterans often feel too pressured or too embarrassed to ask for the help they need to deal with their own deployment related wounds, including the stress, guilt, and despair they may feel for what they may see as abandoning their children during their terms of deployment.

My work with these women is so important to me that I gave up the security of a 20-year public school teaching career to do this.

For me, this is not so much of a sacrifice because, as far as I'm concerned, I am still a teacher, albeit on a different platform— one that gives me the opportunity to serve others in a unique way than I did in the classroom or even in the military.

No matter where I've served, the thing I've always loved the most was seeing the results that are possible when like-minded people come together to work towards a mutually desired goal.

If you're a female veteran who also values (and could use) such camaraderie to help you to find your own breakthroughs, a coach like me can help you.

Or, if you're simply a single-mother who is a worn-out veteran of life's tough knocks, and you're ready to rebuild a new life for you and your children, a coach like me can help you do this too.

If you're in one of these situations, reach out to a coach like me. As you will learn from reading my story, there is no shame in asking for help.

With the help of a personal coach you *can* beat the enemies of stress, guilt, and despair that can imprison you and prevent you from re-connecting and re-imagining your life after completing your military service (or after becoming a single-mom).

Let's do this. And... That's an order!

A Coach Can Help YOU

End Interpersonal Conflicts & Enjoy Happy, Productive, Peaceful Relationships with Family, Friends, & Co-Workers—that will LAST!

Coach Renee Asmar

I'm all about results—quick results.

Since the women and men I work with tend to experience results sooner than expected, most of my clients come to me when they need quicker and longer lasting results.

This means that I only work with clients who are willing to follow through with doing the work needed to achieve the quickest possible results.

People often come to me after procrastinating in getting the help they need. So, by the time they come to me, the delays in tackling the problem have made it worse.

Since I solve interpersonal conflicts, if people delay too long before reaching out to me, they are practically drowning in a sea of turbulence, uncertainty, and havoc by the time I see them.

But, I'm up for the challenge—this is when I tend to do my best work.

The best way to describe what I do for my clients is to let them speak for themselves.

Chapter 5: What Can a Personal Coach Do for YOU?

Here's a small sample of what different clients have repeatedly told me about what they get out of working with me:

> *"So glad I finally decided to stick with it... I wish I had come sooner..."*
>
> *"[I] regret all the months I wasted really being stubborn, afraid, convinced and determined I could do all this on my own; for the unnecessary silent suffering and for what? Like you say, [I'm} taking what I learned, re-claiming my power; the time is now and [I'm] moving forward."*
>
> *"Finally took the step. I am on the right course of action, thank you. I can't believe the difference in my life and work! How I feel different inside; [it] makes a difference in my family, and my department."*
>
> *"The quality of life in our home is happier, productive. I guess I never paid attention to what is really meant by 'fullness of life or having life to the full. Family is everything to me; all the money and command of my time I have means nothing [if I end up] losing my family. To have peace again, my family back in my life, saved me, my health; we're whole again, wouldn't trade it for the world".*

If you're looking to achieve similar results in your family, work, or other areas of life, but you've been putting it off, reach out to me or to another coach.

But, only do it if you're tired of sitting by while things in your life go from bad to worse and you're finally ready to do the work to improve things—*quickly!*

If so, I can help.

In the next chapter, my story explains why helping you make peace with others who matter to you is so important to me. If it connects with you, and you feel we can make peace together, reach out to me.

Until then, I wish you much peace—in every one of your relationships that matter to you.

Chapter 5: *What Can a Personal Coach Do for YOU?*

Chapter Summary & Conclusion

Yes, A Coach Can Help YOU!

Coach D. Forbes-Edelen

As this chapter demonstrates, a coach *can* do a lot for you.

The coaches have shared the ways that they have helped people solve a wide variety of problems and overcome various challenges.

Hopefully, you can now see that working with your own personal coach can help you to achieve some of the same results, including:

- ✓ Achieving goals you may have thought were impossibly out of reach
- ✓ Overcoming personal disappointments that limit the quality of your life
- ✓ Creating lasting, peaceful relationships with those who matter most to you
- ✓ Maintaining the work-life balance needed to become a peak performer in all areas of life
- ✓ Courageously challenging the status quo and breaking free of rules that do not serve you well
- ✓ Shifting your perspective to recognize and maximize your 'inner' beauty

And so much more...

These coaches also made it clear that you can expect them (and any good coach, for that matter), to challenge you, as Coach Haggerty did in her introduction to this chapter.

I am no different.

I also challenge the business owners and entrepreneurs who work with me to make shifts that can be difficult for them.

Among the most difficult of these is shifting from a focus on *selling* their products, services, and ideas, to a focus on *solving* the problems, needs, and concerns of their prospective buyers.

Making this seemingly tiny—but significant—shift can make the difference in whether a business sinks or survives.

Therefore, if I can get my clients to make this shift in thinking, they will shorten the path to business success and close the gap between their ideas and their income.

A problem solving focus gives my clients the confidence to get people to buy what they have to sell without the constant selling, begging, chasing after any and every one—any and everywhere, or hustling for peanuts—that they hate so much.

They stop wasting their precious, but limited, time, money, and energy, trying to get noticed by doing things that can be seductive because it feels good, but that are about as good for the health of their businesses as a constant diet of junk food is for the body.

And, perhaps most important of all, they stop trying to win the race to the bottom by constantly giving away their work for free or throwing away their money on the latest gimmick that comes along but rarely pays off.

While I've worked with a wide-range of business owners and entrepreneurs, I do have a soft-spot for those who are drawn to *quiet* marketing strategies, but feel this puts them at a disadvantage in the noisy and highly competitive marketplace environment of today.

Quiet entrepreneurs tend to over-deliver, but still struggle to get well-paid for the high value they provide because they typically hate to *sell* and dislike *'tooting-their-own-horns' and* so they hesitate to take credit for their accomplishments.

If this sounds like you, then a coach can help you.

With the help of your own personal Business or Marketing coach, you can learn to turn your own unique quirks and so-called weaknesses into opportunities to distinguish your business and create a brand that stands apart and gives you an unfair advantage, even in the current noisy and competitive marketplace.

My own particular brand of genius is helping business owners and entrepreneurs like you to build and sustain profitable businesses by solving problems that make you irreplaceable in the eyes of buyers and then communicating that irreplaceable value (of what you do) more effortlessly.

If this is a result that matters to you, and my story in the next chapter makes us feel like a good fit, then I enthusiastically invite you to reach out to me or to a *Sustainable Marketing Communication* coach like me.

In the next chapter, you will get a chance to learn about the journeys that led each of us to our particular area of specialty and to the people we feel most drawn to helping and serving.

Chapter 6

Meet the Coach

"A coach is defined by his or her journey, and this journey is a window into the transformative possibilities you can co-create"—D. Forbes-Edelen

By
Contributing Coaches

Chapter Introduction
Jayne Logan & D. Forbes-Edelen

In this final chapter, you will get to meet and learn more about the personal stories of each of the contributing coaches and how their individual journeys helped them to discover their coaching specialties and identify the problems they are uniquely positioned to help you solve.

Their journeys are powerful examples of much of the advice they've shared throughout this book.

Getting to know their stories is one of the best ways to understand the kind of transformation you can expect from working with your own coach.

Meet the Coach

Renee Asmar, CPC

Specializing in

Rescuing Relationships in Conflict & Bringing Peace through Connection

My passion is healing and reconciliation.

I help people to manage and heal the conflicts in their personal relationships so they can work productively with others and enjoy peaceful, warm, and loving relationships with those who matter most to them.

I am convinced I was meant to do this from birth.

For as long as I can remember, I've wanted to facilitate healing, reconciliation, and constructive conversation.

I've always had this ache in my stomach whenever I saw people suffering because they were at odds with each other and it always made me feel like I had to do something to bridge the gaps between these people and bring them together.

This became my life's purpose, which is why I became a nun.

But, as satisfying as this career choice was, I wanted to make a bigger impact, beyond the confines of a nun's life-style. So, I searched for other opportunities, outside of the church, to help people make peace with each other.

This search led me to coaching.

It turned out to be a perfect fit for me, and I eventually went on to earn my certification.

Getting certified made me feel better prepared to help individuals who dread waking up in the morning because of the conflict-ridden interactions they were anticipating throughout the day.

Such conflicts can make such ones less productive and cost them their most cherished professional goals, especially when achieving these goals rely on the ability to work closely with people they can't get along with.

As a result, they may feel they have no voice or that their quality of life or the legacy they want to leave behind is diminished.

Surprisingly (and sadly), many times the people struggling most with such interpersonal conflicts are those who seem to have it all, such as business leaders, bosses, and those who are financially well-off.

What makes this sad is that, in spite of their apparent achievements and successes, these people are mostly empty and hurting inside because of the emotional turmoil these destructive interactions and fractured relationships put them through.

I've seen this destructive interpersonal dynamic repeat itself in families, companies, religious orders, schools, churches, communities, organizations, departments, hospitals, clubs, political parties, and among people in conflict-ridden areas of the world.

I want to change this.

Chapter 6: *Meet the Coach*

I actually got my first opportunity to do something about this problem a few years ago in an area that is no stranger to conflict: *The Middle East.*

The danger posed by this challenge was real—so much so that I had to make funeral arrangements, put my affairs in order, and make sure my aging parent would be cared for before I left.

In spite of the danger, I accepted the challenge because of my passion for helping people in conflict to bring peace and reconciliation to their lives.

Once I settled in Israel, I was able to work with men and women from different ethnic, socioeconomic, and religious backgrounds, including Jews, Muslims, Palestinians, Christians, and so on.

I soon discovered that, in spite of these obvious differences, all these people shared common goals that transcended their religious, nationalistic, gender, cultural, or socio-economic differences: *They all cared about their family, the quality of their lives, and their own personal integrity.*

Thus, at their core, they had more in common than they each realized and I was able to use these unifying core desires to bridge the gaps among them.

In an effort to get a real feel for the local people, I had to take the risk of going out in the general population and interacting among the people all by myself.

I genuinely wanted so much to learn from them directly; it was like a fire in my belly. It was so important to me to get a real feel for their heartbeat and for their way of thinking, the risk was worth it.

I began by setting up meetings with the members of these various ethnic and religious groups in different locations and I asked them questions such as:

- *What do you need me to understand about you?*
- *What do you need me to understand about what makes your heart ache?*
- *What are your goals and wishes?*
- *What do you want your legacy to be?*
- *What is it that you would like me, as an American woman, to understand about you?*

As you can imagine, this was not easy.

I had to take a crash course in Hebrew and Arabic so I could communicate with them in their own language, but I felt this was important in order to prove that I was genuinely interested in who *they* were and what was important to *them*.

So with my broken Hebrew, Arabic, my piecemeal French, and my English, I worked hard to engage with these diverse groups of people in any language that made them feel most comfortable.

My hard work paid off.

My efforts to speak their language, even with all my mistakes, put me in good stead. My humility made me approachable and made them see me as non-threatening and safe.

I also gained their trust by dressing in a way that showed them deep respect and proved how much I really cared—because I did.

The lessons I learned during this Middle East adventure are now the cornerstone of my coaching practice.

Chapter 6: *Meet the Coach*

Today I use the same principles, that helped me to bridge the gaps among the diverse religious and ethnic groups in this conflict-ridden area, to help my coaching clients bridge the gaps, mistrusts, and misperceptions that are at the root of the interpersonal conflicts in their own lives.

As it turns out, the conversations that my clients now share with me about the conflicts in their lives sound very similar to the conversations I heard from the groups I listened to while in the Middle East.

It's why after listening intently to them complain about all the things that are not good about those with whom they're in conflict I'm able to help them see these difficult relationships in a new way.

Through the use of observations, questions, and emotional connection I help them to realize that they all want the same thing.

> *Just like themselves, those they are in conflict with also want to live their lives in freedom and harmony, without excessive worry.*

In this way, I lead them to the conclusion that, underneath all the ugliness and darkness of hate and conflict, both sides prefer peace to conflict.

Success in helping such people in conflict see things in this new light depends on my ability to encourage and motivate them to reach out to each other and take the initiative to understand each other's core needs, wants, and goals.

I do this by leveraging the trust they place in me, as their coach, to get them to connect with each other—not just on an intellectual level but on a deeply personal level through direct dialogue and face-to-face conversations in a safe environment. It also requires that, just as those in the Middle East who accepted my invitation to talk had to be committed to the process, in view of the dangers they faced in talking to me, the clients I work with must be equally committed to peace when they work with me.

Such commitment means they have to be willing to put up with some discomfort to achieve the peaceful relationships they want.

But, if they can commit to this process, the end result is that they'll be able to bridge the gaps between themselves and others, through productive dialogue and genuine engagement; thus, they will be able to maintain peaceful relationships in virtually any situation that involves working with people to achieve a common goal.

One of the most unexpected rewards of my work has been helping those at the end stages of their lives to repair the deep anger and hurts they've accumulated over their lifetimes and reconcile with those they care for, before their death; this gives them the closure they need to face death with peace and dignity.

If you're in this end-of-life situation or if you just want to end the conflicts in your life that are undermining your quality of life and work, or robbing you of your peace of mind, productivity, and success, here's a tip I'd like to offer you:

Spend quiet time every day, listening to your inner-self

You see, self-intimacy, which is the ability to tune into your inner self, is a critical first step towards making peace with others (as well as with yourself).

This deceptively simple tip will take work, but the effort is worth it.

Once you're able to connect to your deepest voice and tune into your core essence, you truly become self-generative and your everyday interactions become more peaceful and satisfying.

The opportunity to have such a profound impact on people's lives is the main reason why I am so drawn to coaching.

By allowing me to help those in conflict to bring peace and reconciliation to their lives, coaching allows me to do what I've always felt I was born to do and what my experiences have prepared me to do.

If you could use my help to resolve the conflicts in *your* life, please don't hesitate to reach out to me.

Peace to you…

About the Author. As a specialist in *Personal Peace and Reconciliation*, Renee Asmar helps individuals in conflict to finally heal the hurts, bridge the gaps, and get the interpersonal reconciliations they crave so they can enjoy the greater financial success, better health, end of life peace, and improved productivity that comes from getting along and working well with co-workers, family members, and friends. She can be reached by email at reneecpcoach@gmail.com or by phone at 914.570.4748.

Meet the Coach

Cynthia Chevrestt, CPC

Specializing in

Helping Female Veterans (& Other Women) Overcome the Guilt and Despair of Single-Motherhood so They Can Create a GREAT New Life

As a Certified Professional Coach (CPC) who works with single-mothers in transition, my primary focus is working with women veterans.

I help these women to successfully transition from the military to civilian life, without the guilt, depression and self-sabotage that often stops them from thriving after ending their military careers.

Many female veterans struggle with some of the same issues as their male counterparts (such as homelessness and unemployment), when they try to reconnect with the civilian world.

But, unlike their male counterparts, women veterans (especially single-mothers) bear the extra burden of having to shoulder, all by themselves, the full responsibility of handling the household labor while caring for children and trying to find a way to make a decent living after they return home.

It's not surprising that they experience higher levels of Post-Traumatic Stress Disorder (PTSD), sexual violence, and depression than women in the general population or that they

Chapter 6: Meet the Coach

commit suicide at nearly six times the rate of other women who have never served in the military.

I was one of these at-risk female veterans.

I've experienced the feelings of disconnection, depression, and guilt that comes from carrying the burden of managing a household, caring for children, and trying to make a decent living for my family, all by myself.

From personal experience, therefore, I know how little help is available for these vulnerable women and this is why I created my *Winning Formula* program, called:

> *The Winning Formula to a GREAT Life: A Complete Life Shift from Just Getting by and Surviving to Thriving.*

In this program, I've put together all of the most useful insights I've learned from my own journey from depression and despair to connection and contentment.

It was born from the rubbles of my own breakdown.

The breakthroughs that led to the creation of this program came one morning on my way to a Goal Setting Workshop.

As I started to leave my teenage children that early morning, I suddenly froze.

I started to remember the stress, guilt, anguish, and depression I had quietly struggled with inside of me since they were young and I had to leave them in the care of others (both strangers and their unsupportive father), while I went away on military duty—sometimes for as long as 18-months.

In the blink of an eye, the feelings of guilt over what I felt was an abandonment of my children (which I really thought was behind me), came crashing down on me like a two-ton weight on a flea.

I felt like a failure as a mother. I felt so incredibly alone.

Yet, I was too embarrassed to share my internal struggles with anyone or ask for help. I kept beating up on myself and telling myself that I was a soldier and that I should just toughen up and handle it! It didn't help.

I cried that morning like I had never cried before.

All the pent-up despair that I had stuffed inside of me during 10 years of military duty erupted that morning like an avalanche.

This was the beginning of an emotional storm that lasted several distressing days before I was finally forced to face up to the guilt and regrets I had stuffed down inside of me, over all the lost years and missed firsts that I was not there to share with my children.

After a while, though, I started to emerge from the storm and when I did, something amazing started to happen.

I call it an awakening because it led to a life-changing breakthrough that turned my life around.

It suddenly hit me that I was actually punishing myself for the wrongs I felt I had done to my kids and that I was self-sabotaging my efforts to create a financially secure future because I didn't feel I deserved to be successful.

Even more shocking to me, I also realized that I was trying to compensate for my guilt by being over-indulgent with my kids—not saying no to them and sparing nothing to give them whatever they wanted—just so they would like me.

Of course, once I realized what I was doing, I also knew that if I didn't stop it, I would destroy the two things I loved the most:

My children and my life.

With this realization, my thinking shifted. I actually felt re-energized, like I had found a new purpose in life.

I poured this newfound energy into creating a series of audios to capture my thoughts in real time so I could hear them and openly confront them and talk back to those self-critical thoughts that had gone unchallenged for far too long.

The more I talked back, the more powerful I felt.

These audio recordings eventually became the basis for my *Winning Formula* coaching program.

The goal of this program is to help those vulnerable women veterans, especially those single-mothers who are now where I used to be, to get rid of the guilt that is one of the biggest obstacles that's stopping them from creating the successful post-military life they truly want and deserve.

If you're one of these women,

I can tell you that, once you're able to conquer this cancerous guilt that almost destroyed me, and that I've seen destroy so many lives, it can make a profound difference in your life.

For instance,

Getting rid of this guilt can mean that,

- You (and your children) will finally be able to more deeply connect, form unbreakable bonds with each other, and more fully thrive—whether you're together or apart.

- You'll be able to find new financially enriching opportunities to apply the skills, focus, and discipline you developed in your military career towards creating the dream career you want, so you can stop being constantly weighed down by the strain of worrying about making ends meet.

- You'll have the emotional energy and stamina to raise your kids to be the happy, healthy, productive, and successful adults you want them to become without feeling like you have to constantly give in to your kids' demands to make up for being the bad mother you're wrongly convinced you are.

- You'll be able to unapologetically look for the loving partner you want, without the baggage of feeling like you're undeserving, being selfish, or that you have to apologize for wanting more and better things for yourself.

As you can see from my experience, I am able to help you achieve these results quicker and with less heartache than it cost me because I've been there.

I know what it takes to rebuild a life from the rubbles of a breakdown and I know how to survive the transition from deployment to re-engagement in civilian life, with less friction and strife than trying to do it on your own.

And, I know how hard it can be do ask for help.

But, I encourage you to do it.

Chapter 6: *Meet the Coach*

Once I admitted that I needed help and I became as committed to getting help as I was to my military missions, it made all the difference in the world for me.

This was when my transformation really began. And, it can do the same for you.

My help came in the form of a coach who helped me to move forward by guiding me through the process of moving from discovering my purpose (to help women veterans with struggles like my own), to taking the actions necessary to make this purpose a reality.

What I've been able to accomplish after going through this process has been priceless; it's now the same kind of transformation I want to bring to the lives of other veterans and single-mothers who may be going through their own breakdown (or just emerging from one), and are now ready to bring their own dreams and passions to life.

Since I want to positively impact the lives of as many people as possible, and I love the camaraderie of working towards a common goal with a group of like-minded people, I primarily help these women through group programs and retreats.

I've found that there is an uncommon bond among the community of women in my retreats and group programs that we women veterans and single-mothers cannot find anywhere else.

This unconditional positive support, which is such an integral part of my programs and retreats, is a big reason why the women who work with me are able to get the results they want faster and maintain their success longer than they can on their own.

My dream is that, with my help, no woman veteran or single-mother will ever have to feel alone again as they go through their own journey from breakdown to breakthrough.

About the Author. Cynthia Chevrestt is a *Veteran & Life Transition Coach*, who specializes in helping women veterans and single mothers create the GREAT life they want. Through her *Winning Formula* coaching programs and retreats, she helps these women lose the guilt so they can successfully transition from the military to civilian life or from being a couple to being a single mother—without feeling like they're undeserving, being selfish, or have to apologize for wanting more and better things for themselves (and their children). She can be reached by phone at 954-695-4686 or online at LiveAGreatLife.net.

Meet the Coach

D. Forbes-Edelen, CPC

Specializing in

Helping Entrepreneurs & Business Owners Find the Right Words to Sell More of their Services, Ideas, & Products with Elegance & Ease

My particular brand of genius is helping entrepreneurs and business owners effortlessly make money for what they do.

I learned the art of effortless entrepreneurship from my mother, who I watched run a successful home-based business with joy, elegance, and ease.

It never seemed like running her business was a struggle. The house just always seemed to be bustling with a fun energy as she created her products and served her clients.

It's probably not surprising, then, that I would soon follow in her footsteps, by creating and selling my own profit-making service at 7 years old.

It happened quite accidentally one lazy fall evening just before sundown.

I was just laying on the grass with a group of bored neighborhood kids, with pockets full of change in anticipation of the arrival of our favorite snack truck, when something caught my attention.

Out of the corner of my eye, I noticed one child playing with some cut-out paper figures and it sparked an idea.

A short time later, I had written a script, created more cut-out characters, recruited a few neighborhood kids to play the parts, and, just like that, my first business was born.

My marketing strategy was simple: *I sold my service as an experience that gave bored kids something cool to do.*

For a penny, they could buy a back seat to see my show and for two pennies, those who could find a flashlight could buy front row seats that gave them a special role in the show:

> They would be allowed to shine their flashlights to light up the sheets that served as the imaginary screen where we watched the animated silhouettes of the paper dolls come alive.

So it was, that as easy as child's play, I was able to turn an unrecognized opportunity to fill an unmet need into a profitable business. I've been doing some version of this ever since.

As an adult, the entrepreneurial seed that was planted by my mother and my early taste of business success grew as I worked for (and with), money-making powerhouses like *Walt Disney, Sheraton Hotels, Smith-Barney, and Paine-Webber;* and, as I earned my degrees in communication and marketing and ran a successful marketing communication consultant agency.

Eventually, my love of learning led me to pursue a doctorate degree. But, while I loved helping students master new skills, I never felt as comfortable within the constraints of the college classroom as I felt while starting, improving, or growing a business—or helping someone else to do so.

Truly, these entrepreneurial challenges are how I breathe.

Chapter 6: Meet the Coach

It seems obvious now, but it took me a while to turn this self-insight into a business coaching career.

The slow epiphany began with my husband's massive stroke, one beautiful day during spring-break, while I was in the final stages of completing my doctorate degree.

The difficulties imposed by his illness and recovery soon made it impossible for me to complete my degree. I was forced to quit and it made me feel like such a failure.

While I now see it as a gift when life forces you off a path that may not be right for you, at the time I was overcome with debilitating shame and bitter disappointment at not being able to muster up whatever character strength it took to just finish.

I was able to recover by doing the same thing I did as a 7-year old entrepreneur. I started to look around for opportunities to fill unmet needs in my backyard.

I took notice of struggling local business owners and reached out to help them with their marketing messages, business operations, and media buying needs.

Then I volunteered with local business development organizations to help them mentor, support, and advise the local business owners they served.

This triggered a desire to earn my coaching certification.

But, although my business coaching specialty seems obvious now, I didn't discover the obvious until I went through the process of being coached, as a requirement for earning my certification.

Before this, I had been minimizing the value of my particular brand of genius for business and marketing because it was just something I did as easy as child's play. In spite of all the

evidence to the contrary, I had somehow convinced myself that any talent that came so easily for me could not possibly be of much value to anyone.
Go figure.

If you are also in the habit of minimizing the value of your own unique talents, get a coach.

As my coach did for me, the right coach can really help you to value and actualize your own genius, so you can turn it into a prosperous career doing work you love and can be proud of.

If you decide that the work you love is to make money by turning your particular brand of genius into a business and you could use my help to grow your business with more elegance and ease, reach out to me.

It would make my day to help you build a profitable business you can sustain with less begging, selling, or chasing after any and every one (any and everywhere) just to work for peanuts.

About the Author. As a *Marketing Communication* specialist, D. Forbes-Edelen helps growth-oriented business owners & entrepreneurs generate sustainable profits by solving the right problems and communicating the irreplaceable value of what they do to the right buyers—with elegance and ease. She can be reached online at: ILoveMarketingWithoutSelling.com

Meet the Coach

Julie Haggerty, CPC

Specializing in

Helping Ambitious People Who Think they're Not Good Enough or Smart Enough—to Turn their Dreams of a Healthcare Career into a Reality

As a healthcare career development coach, I work with people who want to pursue a healthcare career but are struggling to figure out which healthcare path is right for them.

This coaching specialty is the result of my own journey.

Some folks spring out of bed each morning knowing exactly what they want to do in life. But, far too many others play the wishing game.

They grudgingly flop out of bed, head in hands, dreading the day before them, and *wishing* for a savior to come along and deliver them from the unsatisfying consequences of the choices they've made in life—choices that's led them where they don't want to be.

Then there are those who go through life *wishing* they'd just win the lottery and all their problems would be solved.

If you're playing your own version of the wishing game, you're not alone. A few years ago, I was doing the same thing.

But, my grandmother used to say two things that helped me—and they can help you too.

She told me,

> "Wishin' don't bring home the bacon. You gotta be the driver of your own train."
>
> "It's fine to talk to yourself—if it's the only way you can get a good answer."

Let me translate.

The point of my grandma's wonderfully eccentric advice is this:

> Getting what you want requires action and talking to someone you can trust to give you good answers.

So, if you want to map out the path to your dream career, you've got to stop wishing and start talking to the right person—preferably to a coach.

It was by following her advice that I was able to achieve my own dream of becoming a registered nurse—although, I changed paths in mid-stream several times and jumped from one area of the healthcare field to another before I finally accomplished it.

I want to help you to learn from my mistakes so you can stop playing the *wishing game* and start working in a fulfilling career much sooner than I did, and without all the wasted time and money that it cost me to get there.

Perhaps you already enjoy helping people and you've just decided that a healthcare career is right for you, but you aren't sure if it's best to test the waters by working as a nursing assistant first to see if nursing is really a good fit for you.

Chapter 6: Meet the Coach

Or, maybe you're already an experienced LNA (or licensed nursing assistant) who's worried that you'll not be able to increase your salary above a certain cap, as a nurses' aide, but you're anxious about taking the next step to advance your career.

If either of these describe your situation, I have one question for you: *What are you going to do about it?*

In turn, you may want to ask *me* a couple of questions, like:

> *What choice do I have—especially since I just can't quit my job to go to school?*

Or,

> *Where do I even start?*

This is where I come in.

As a healthcare career coach, I am your career tour guide, mentor, and brainstorming partner.

Regardless of the role I play, I can help you to reach your healthcare career goal without having to take the long and expensive, stop-and-start path I took because I didn't have the kind of help I can give to you.

Since I really didn't know that there was such a thing as a life coach and I certainly didn't understand what a valuable asset a coach could have been to me, I had to figure it all out on my own.

If you're in the same position and, for whatever reason, you're not working with a coach, I'll share the one thing I did that helped me when I didn't have a coach—and may help you too.

I developed an informal buddy system.

This buddy system consisted of a few family, friends, and acquaintances who could help me to keep going during those times when I was full of doubt and uncertainty and felt the most adrift. It became the bridge I needed to get from where I was to where I wanted to be.

So, other than working with a coach of your own, developing a buddy system can be one of the next best thing you can do for yourself.

As a healthcare career coach, I am the buddy that can help you bridge that gap from dreaming of a healthcare career to making a living as a healthcare professional.

Some of the roadblocks you'll face along the way include,

- Uncertainty about how to get started
- Indecision about which is the right training program for you
- Figuring out who you can rely on to hold you accountable when you're tempted to give up

Based on my personal experience and my work with clients, I've found that the most critical of these roadblocks to overcome is the last one.

You need an accountability partner to keep you on track; believe me, a pound of accountability can spur a ton of growth.

Your own personal coach is an invaluable accountability partner, especially if you're one of those who habitually tell yourself:

> I'm Not Good or Smart Enough.

I struggled with these exact feelings as I pursued by own healthcare career.

Chapter 6: *Meet the Coach*

I also had to deal with very challenging circumstances. At the time, I had two children under 4 years old.

My eldest, who had been diagnosed with Autism at 2 years old, and my youngest, who was himself, now a healthy, but precocious and energetic two-year-old.

We had to move to a small rural town several hundred miles away to get my autistic daughter the help she needed to have the best possible chance at a good life well into the future.

However, since my husband's income was our only means of support, he couldn't quit his job, which meant he had to travel back and forth between our two states, returning home one or two days each week. Thus, for the most part, I had to care for our children alone.

The situation was made even more challenging because I didn't know how to drive.

Without a driver's license I had to wait for my husband to return home once or twice each week to do basic tasks like get groceries and get to the local laundromat.

During this difficult time, I spent a lot of time in the **Wishing Well.**

> I was *wishing* that my daughter wasn't autistic; I was *wishing* I could drive; I *was wishing* my husband didn't have to travel so far to work; and I was *wishing* we had more money.

Finally, I took my grandma's advice and I stopped wishing and started doing.

First, I got my daughter settled in her development program and placed my son into a subsidized daycare.

Next, I set my sights on getting my driver's license.

My husband didn't have the time or the inclination to teach me to drive and we couldn't waste money on paying for driving lessons, so I did the next best thing:

> I took an old beat up car (or what we call, in my neck of the woods, a *Hunk 'O Junk*) that was in our yard, and I taught myself to drive.

First, I taught myself to drive around the park. After a couple of weeks, I got up the nerve to drive on the scary two-lane main road nearby.

My first attempt was so terrifying I immediately turned around, got back to my front yard, parked the car, and swore I would never get in that death trap again.

But I didn't give up.

The next morning, I went out again. This time, I went a little farther and a little farther after that. Before I knew it, I was able to drive myself to the local shopping mall and post office.

I was so proud of myself after this accomplishment, it motivated me to schedule my road test. And, with the support of a dear friend who loaned me her car for the test, I passed that road test.

I will never forget my friend's act of kindness and her belief in me. Her kindness gave me confidence that I could do it.

Once I got my driver's license, I was unstoppable.

Accomplishing that one goal gave me the confidence to know that I could set a goal, work a plan, and follow it through to completion. Knowing this about myself spurred me on to my next goal and the next, and set the stage for many more achievements throughout my life.

This is why I want to help you to get your first taste of success so you too can develop the same confidence in your ability to set your own goals and take the actions necessary to achieve them.

Once I had my driver's license, the world opened up to me. I was now able to look for work.

However, since I only had my GED, I was only being offered minimum wage retail jobs, one of which I took because we needed the money.

My next career move was to drive a school bus. I took this job because I couldn't afford daycare for my son and the bus company allowed me to take him along, as long as I provided a car seat to place him in.

Score! I thought. No daycare fees meant more money coming into my household.

Yet, quite unexpectedly, driving the school bus introduced me to my next career.

While picking kids up and dropping them off around the neighborhood, I started to notice the *For Sale* signs all around the neighborhood.

They sparked my imagination.

I began to think about selling houses. I imagined getting my real estate license and bringing home good money while working a flexible schedule and having more time with my kids.

Eventually, I moved from imagining it to doing it. I became a Real Estate agent.

After a few years, though, I was disillusioned. The income fell far short of what I had hoped, and most of all, it just wasn't fulfilling, so I began to search for my next career.

The chance came when I saw an ad for a Certified Nursing Assistant (CNA) course.

I can still remember how happy I felt just thinking about the course and all the future possibilities that a being a certified healthcare professional would offer me.

When I saw that ad, it brought me back to when I was a teen and used to volunteer at a rehabilitation hospital. I loved every minute of it because, as a teenager, I used to dream of becoming a nurse.

But, this dream came to a screeching halt at sixteen years old, with the sudden death of my father.

One day, my father, the light of our home, was diagnosed with Hodgkin's Lymphoma; a year later, he was dead.

My life took a different turn; I was sidetracked from the healthcare career I had dreamed of so much.

I had to quit high school and go to work fulltime to help my mother and brothers, who were not yet old enough to go out to work. I started working in retail jobs. Eventually, I was promoted to head of accounts payable and receivable, which came with a pay raise that was decent money for the time.

Then, at 19 years old, I got married and the children came.

Chapter 6: *Meet the Coach*

We were financially okay for a while—but something was still missing for me. I kept dreaming about that nursing career I had envisioned for myself for so long.

As the years went on, my dreams were replaced by an accusing finger that kept poking at me and by nagging thoughts that kept berating me, saying,

> *'You're too old now. Your time has passed. You're not smart enough. It's too hard. It'll take too long. Just be happy with your lot and stop thinking about that old, dead dream of becoming a nurse.'*

This constant internal scolding took its toll. I eventually gave up on my dream of becoming a nurse.

That's why when I saw the ad for the CNA course, it breathed new life into my dream—and into me.

I answered it and went on to become the nurse I had wanted to be since I was a teenager.

Since then, I've spent many fulfilling decades as a nurse, until recently, as new developments in the healthcare industry have increasingly pushed nurses away from the hands-on patient care that I loved so much.

These industry changes triggered a few personal challenges that led me to discover a new calling: *Life Coaching*.

It was the answer to the one flaw I discovered with the informal buddy system.

I came to realize that, although I benefited from the support of great friends and mentors to get through many personal and professional challenges, their support was often not enough to light the fire under me that I needed to get me where I wanted to go.

If this has happened to you too, it's not your fault.

This failure occurs because it is so hard for our dear friends to be objective. Their lack of objectivity will cause them to either hold back from telling us the truth in order to preserve the friendship, or it will make them so afraid of being left behind when we achieve our goals that they will feed that little voice in our heads that tells us, *you can't do it!*

That's why turning to a Life Coach can make such a difference.

I wish I knew this years ago.

If I had, I know it would not have taken me 7 years to get a 2-year nursing degree—even if you may be thinking,

> *Are you kidding me? It's completely unrealistic to think that you could complete a rigorous nursing degree in 2 years—with all the things you had on your plate at the time. For goodness sakes, you were a wife who was running a home with 2 young kids, one with special needs, while at the same time you were holding down a fulltime job.*

While I don't disagree with these thoughts, based on what I know now, I can say with absolute certainty that, even with all I had on my plate, I could still have reached my goal in half the time, if I had worked with a personal coach.

So, my point is that, without the help of a coach who could brainstorm ideas with me and help me clear my mind of all the head trash that kept stopping me from moving forward, I made many avoidable mistakes that cost me a lot of time, money, stress.

That's why it's now my dream to help others to reach their own dreams of a healthcare career, much sooner that I did and with less cost.

If this is you, I don't want you to become side-tracked by the twists and turns of your life. I don't want the obstacles that life throws in your path to bring you to a standstill. I want you to keep moving towards your goal, no matter what. And, I want to be the one to help you get there by leading you past the obstacles and helping you take the correct steps to make your healthcare career dreams a reality.

As my journey proves, you can do it—regardless of the many starts and stops you'll encounter along the way.

My own struggles have given me the experience, knowledge, expertise, and most importantly, the desire to assist you on your journey to building the healthcare career that you've been dreaming of and that you're uniquely destined for. I invite you to reach out to me, if you could use my help.

About the Author. Julie Haggerty is a *Healthcare Career Development Coach* who works with underserved and disadvantaged adult students with challenging life circumstances, who dream of getting into the healthcare field and having a successful healthcare career, but feel they are not good enough or smart enough to achieve this goal. She helps them to overcome both self-imposed and other barriers their life circumstances have imposed on them so they can build the successful healthcare career they want, earn the higher income they long for, and enjoy the lasting career satisfaction they deserve for their hard work. She can be reached by email at: julhag@hotmail.com.

Meet the Coach

Fran Holinda, CPC

Specializing in

Helping Women over 50 Make the Shift to See the Beauty Within them & Seize the Opportunities Life Offers them— At Any Age

As a Perspectives Coach, I most often work with women over 50-years of age to help them improve the quality of their lives by learning to see situations from a new perspective.

This is much more than trying to get them to move from a glass half empty to a glass half full philosophy.

The *Perspective Shift* that I help these women to make is to move from focusing on the negative aspect of any problem or obstacle they face to focusing on the specific positive outcome they want to achieve.

I do not believe in a one size fits all approach; I am unique and so are each of my clients. This is why my coaching program is designed for women who want and value highly customizable, individualized attention.

This approach comes out of my own experience.

Unlike many life coaches whose coaching specialties are born out of great personal struggles and tragedy, I've been fortunate enough in my life to have never had to overcome a major illness or great personal tragedy.

Chapter 6: Meet the Coach

At first, my fairly problem-free background made me feel that I hadn't suffered enough to have anything of real value to offer my coaching clients.

After all, as you well know, in our society people tend to be drawn to survivors and high-achievers who have beaten great odds rather than to just ordinary folks, like me.

That's why the biggest obstacle I had to overcome when I decided to become a coach was self-doubt.

I wasn't sure that I really had anything to offer and I wondered if there was a role in coaching for someone like me, who was just an ordinary person with only a gift for coaching and a heart for helping others.

Before I share how I was able to put these doubts to rest, let me return to the beginning of my journey, which began when I turned fifty.

In celebration of this milestone, I gave myself the gift of joining a fitness boot-camp.

Soon, I was hooked.

It wasn't so much the physical transformation that hooked me; it was the way getting fit made me feel about myself.

In a short time, I became less stressed, had more energy, and felt more youthful and revitalized.

When I experienced the unbelievable impact the boot-camp trainer had on me and others in the program, I knew that I wanted to be in a profession where I could have the same transformative impact on people's lives.

Not surprisingly, I decided to become a personal trainer.

Not too long after making the decision, I had not only earned my certification as a NASM Certified Personal Trainer (the most well-known and highly respected certification in this industry), but I also had my first part-time job in fitness; and with that, my new fitness career was born.

However, before long it became clear that the one-size fits all personal training approach just wasn't for me.

The singular focus on the outward appearance, without any real attention to the way people felt about themselves made me feel that I was doing my fitness clients a disservice.

You see, for me, the most important part of my work as a personal trainer was not the physical work I did with clients, it was the internal work we did during the personalized, albeit informal, coaching that I gave them. This is what produced the most satisfying results for me, and the most lasting transformations for them.

Accordingly, to more accurately reflect what I was actually doing for clients, I added *life coaching* to my fitness services.

After nearly two years of going all out and pouring almost all of my money and energy into this new value-added service, it became clear that it was not resonating with people. In fact, I was confusing them by offering life coaching services when they were coming to me for fitness training.

This is when I decided to become certified as a Professional Life Coach.

This training was priceless—not just because of the invaluable techniques and methods I learned, but because of the unexpected insights I discovered about myself. The most valuable of these was the realization that I didn't have to suffer to be a good coach.

I realized that I had a lot offer just the way I was, and that I could have the positive impact on people's lives that I longed to have, just by being myself.

As eye-opening as this insight was, the real clarity about the value I had to offer came from probing my group of friends who had worked with their own coaches.

After asking each of them to tell me the one thing that they got from working with a coach, the most enlightening response was that working with a coach *"helped me put things in perspective."*

This response was a light-bulb moment for me. It made me suddenly know what I was meant to do and who I was meant to serve.

For the first time since I started my second-act, at 50, I finally understood why being a personal trainer had not been satisfying to me. It now made sense to me why I was so drawn to working with clients on their internal selves instead of just their outward appearances.

It became crystal clear to me that my life had prepared me to help others like me make their own perspective shifts, as I had done. This is why I was meant to be a coach and it's what my specialty as a *Perspectives Coach* allows me to do every day.

Now, I no longer get irritated at people who refuse to spend the same time and money on their internal development as they spend on their outward appearance.

Instead, I focus on working with women who already recognize the value of falling in love with who they are on the inside, but just cannot make this internal perspective shift alone.

Making this shift is not easy to do; it is a deeply personal journey that requires committed effort, so by coaching these women past the obstacles preventing them from making this shift, I make a real difference in their lives.

If you're at a stage now where you're trying to shift your own perspective on your life, I can assure you that it *is* worth the effort.

Once you shift from being angry and upset because your life isn't the way it should be, and instead begin to recognize and seize the opportunities in front of you to create the life you want, it will transform the way you see yourself, your life, and your legacy.

It will make you feel just as unstoppable as I now feel. That's why it is the one gift I want to give to you.

This is what motivated me to move from taking the ridiculous amounts of money people threw at me to help them look fabulous on the outside, to now helping discerning people like you, who value inner beauty, to look fabulous from the inside-out.

My approach works best for those who demand more from themselves—and *for* themselves.

I'll be the first to admit that my coaching journey has been extremely frustrating at times, but the rewards have made these frustrations pale into insignificance.

Few careers allow you to make the profound impact on people's lives that coaching does.

After a few less than fulfilling careers, it's an unending high to have finally found one that allows me to help so many people achieve meaningful success, just by being who I am.

Interestingly, I've wanted to be a teacher from the time I was 5 years old. I used to pretend I was grading papers by making stars on pieces of paper with my crayons.

So, I suppose that coaching is my way of teaching, with the difference being that I don't talk *at* students and *tell* them what they should know.

Instead, I have the more rewarding task of talking *with* clients and helping them to discover what they already know and express who they already are.

About the Author. Fran Holinda is a *Perspective Coach*. She works with women in their 50s and older who want more for themselves in their second act of life, and are ready to make it their priority to seize the opportunities available for them to do so. She helps them create a life after 50 that makes them feel beautiful inside and out so they can be more independent, self-reliant, as well as more financially and personally enriched as they live out the second part of their lives. She can be reached at PerspectivesLifeCoaching.com

Meet the Coach

Jayne Logan, CPC

Specializing in

*Helping Enlightened Professionals & Leaders
Create Purposeful Lives & Meaningful, Satisfying Careers
by Understanding that Transformation IS the Journey—
NOT the destination*

Before I tell you my story, I'd like to introduce you to Esther.

> Esther was a 58 year-old woman when she approached me in a state of despair.
>
> She felt unhappy and lost because her life was a non-stop cycle of poor choices and self-recriminations. By the time I met her, she had resigned herself to accepting that this was just the way her life was meant to be.
>
> She had so little self-confidence that she thought any decision she made (no matter how small) would be wrong or would make things worse, and so she lived her life in a constant state of paralysis and inaction.
>
> The thing that was most confounding about her situation was that she had so many lovely gifts that she just couldn't see. She literally could not name one positive thing about herself. The only thing she could say about herself was that she was "useless" and "no good at anything."
>
> Yet, in just a few months after we started working together, Esther was able to turn around these self-defeating patterns of a lifetime.

Chapter 6: *Meet the Coach*

Before I tell you how we were able to do this, let me explain how I became a coach in the first place.

My story began exactly three weeks before my 51st birthday.

The date is etched in my memory because it was the day my mother died, barely three weeks after we learned she had Pancreatic Cancer. It was also my dad's 77th Birthday.

As you can imagine, I was heartbroken and inconsolable.

I couldn't stop thinking of all the things she would miss out on. I thought about all the things she still wanted to see but never would; all the places she wanted to go but wouldn't be able to; and all the things she wanted to do but would never be able to accomplish.

I also thought of the grandchildren she wouldn't see grow up and the many other things that were so dear to her that she would never again experience and enjoy.

Then, as I recalled many of the conversations we'd had over the years, I realized how many things she wanted to do but didn't because of the choices she made—primarily the choice to put her children first.

Her three children were the only things she wanted most out of life—having us was the one desire that she was willing to put everything else second to fulfill. In fact, she even wanted more children, but *settled* for the three of us.

Reflecting on the choices my mother made, and how they shaped her life, led me on a journey of my own—a quest for purpose—if you will.

My quest took me in many different directions.

I read dozens of books on subjects like spirituality, human consciousness, and other related topics. I attended seminars and traveled to Europe, Australia and across North America, all in order to expand my perspective and gain deeper insights about what next to do with my life.

I took stock of the many opportunities and experiences I've had and the people I've had the good fortune of learning from, one of whom was a long-time mentor and friend.

During a life-changing conversation with him about the body of work we had amassed together over the years, I had an epiphany that led to my decision to become a coach.

Our conversation helped me to realize that I didn't want to take all the knowledge I had accumulated over the years with me when I left this earth. It became clear to me that I would not be satisfied with my life unless I could figure out how to translate my experiences into something that would make a real difference for others.

After some more soul-searching and digging, I concluded that the only way I could satisfy this imperative was to become a coach.

Since I had this insight, I've been able to turn my decades of business, sales, leadership development, management and Human Resources experiences, into a coaching business that helps others in profound ways.

But, probably even more important to me, my coaching career has allowed me to honor my mother for the positive influence she had on me with her life-long love, unconditional support and good humor.

And, now that my father has since died, making a difference through my coaching matters to me even more.

Chapter 6: *Meet the Coach*

It matters to me because the difference I make with my life is my personal eulogy to my parents. It is my way of saying that their love, sacrifices, and the lessons they passed on to me—all the reasons for their having been here—truly mattered.

Losing my parents taught me that nothing is forever, so I know that coaching may not be my ultimate *final* destination; still, it is an important part of my journey that I fully embrace right now.

In view of the transiency of life, I want to get my clients to their goals quickly—with the least amount of wasted time, energy, and resources.

And, since I view the way I live my life as my parents' legacy, this purpose-driven focus drives me to fully commit to clients in a way that builds instant trust and creates a climate of support. This is what helped *Esther* (who I introduced at the beginning of my story), to transform her life so quickly after we started working together.

Let me explain how we did it.

Our first challenge was identifying what she really wanted out of life. This was harder than it sounds because of her lifetime habit of self-defeatist thinking.

Just like my own experience of trying to figure out what was next for me, Esther also had to go on her own journey of discovery to figure this out for herself. The fact is, when we first started working together, she knew more about what she didn't want (had lots of examples of these), than what she did want.

Our discovery work centered on figuring out what goals mattered to her so much that it would motivate her to really want to change her habitually self-defeating patterns.

In addition to our weekly face-to-face meetings, I created customized real-life situational exercises for her as homework assignments.

Soon, she began to experience some small wins which, over time, became a powerful collection of positive successes that boosted her confidence, re-energized her, and had her believing in herself again.

As her wins mounted, she began reaching out to others and initiating interactions on her own; these were so positive, she started to trust her own decisions.

As she gained momentum, Esther no longer needed to borrow my belief in her to motivate herself, as she did when we first started working together. Now she started to believe in herself and could more easily see the possibilities open to her.

Within about 6-months of this practical, focused, customized, coaching program, I had the pleasure of hearing her say,

> *"I am happier than I've been since I can remember, and I feel an excitement I never expected to feel again."*

In this short time, Esther went from someone who could not make a decision, to a confident, self-assured woman who was able to confidently make BIG decisions, like the one she made to sell the house she had lived in so unhappily for 25 years, to move into a condo that did not drain her energy or resources.

The successful outcome of this one BIG decision gave her confidence to move forward, take control of her life, and make things happen because she had now proven to herself that she *could* make important decisions successfully.

The next goal we're working on now is creating a retirement career for herself.

Since this goal is very similar to my own quest for what's next after the loss of my parents, I know I can help her in this next phase of her life.

This client's transformation has been thrilling to see. But, knowing that I was instrumental in making it happen is what gives my life new meaning; it's the reason I do this work.

This is just one example of the type of life-affirming difference that I'm all about creating in people's lives; and, it's the type of results that drive my coaching philosophy, which is:

> *There is **always** a way, <u>IF</u> you are committed.*

In practice, this means that when (as coaches often do), I work with clients who are skeptical that they can get the results they want because their past life experiences have taught them to doubt their abilities, it is my job—indeed my duty—to challenge these taken-for-granted assumptions, without making my clients feel judged.

For example, if my client says *"Nothing I've tried has ever worked."*

I'll ask this client to finish this statement by adding, *"Up until now."*

Adding this simple phrase is powerful because it reframes their self-defeating assumptions about themselves into a more positive statement that they *can* actually accept as true for them.

It works because it validates the truth of their experiences, without making it seem as if I'm making judgments about them, making them wrong, or minimizing their experiences.

This judgment-free reframing can work for you too. Try it. It will give you permission to start new and take the first step towards putting the past behind you. It will create mental space for you so you can consider the new idea that, you *can* change and you *can* achieve things you may think are impossible for you.

Once you begin to see this light of possibility at the end of a lifelong tunnel of doubt, it is much easier to start trusting and believing in yourself, even if it's for the first time in your life.

Of course this work is far from easy; but it is *doable*—and, it's rewarding (for us both).

However, my work goes beyond just helping individuals.

I also specialize in *Personal, Career, & Leadership Development*, which allows me to make an even bigger difference in many more lives by coaching organizational and corporate leaders, managers, supervisors, and staff.

When organizational leaders are more confident and capable, they are able to build more engaged teams that will more consistently meet or exceed key business metrics—with less struggle. And, since the tangible and intangible benefits of such a productive workforce will ripple throughout the entire organization, my work gets to positively impact more lives.

My experience shows that, whether working with individuals or large groups, people are unique.

Every client comes to their coach with a different frame of reference forged by their unique life experiences, cultural influences, and circumstances. This is why it's critical for a coach to understand that there is no such thing as a one-size-fits-all approach.

Sure, there may be similarities between the goals of different clients, but every individual is unique and so too must the coaching approach be—if it is to be truly effective for each person or organization.

A coach's ability to make this distinction is both the joy and the challenge of coaching. Meeting this challenge successfully is what makes the rewards of coaching so sweet.

About the Author. Jayne Logan is a *Personal & Career Transition and Leadership Development Coach* who helps new and seasoned professionals create careers that are aligned with their strengths so they can fulfill their potential, and enjoy rewarding and satisfying careers and personal lives. She also helps managers, supervisors, and other organizational leaders, more confidently and competently lead highly functioning and engaged teams that consistently meet or exceed organizational goals, and complete assigned projects on time and on budget. She can be reached online at MyOptimumLife.ca or by phone at 416-540-5681.

Meet the Coach

Jen Ryan, CPC

Specializing in

Helping Women Balance Work & Career by Becoming Successful at the RIGHT things so they can Perform at their Peak at Home, Work, Play, & Business

I've always known that everyone has a specific purpose.

I suppose that's why, even though I was the youngest of 8 children, I never felt overshadowed by my siblings or jealous of their accomplishments. There was always a *knowing* inside of me that just made me sure there was a special place in this world for me.

I really can't explain this *knowing*.

It wasn't something that we discussed in my family. It's just something I knew I had—and that I assumed everyone had.

Looking back at it now, I guess it might have just been my version of faith—that strong belief that there was something bigger out there for me to accomplish.

This may be the reason why I was always drawn to the old-souls and wise ones in my life rather than to those my own age, who were younger, but inexperienced and untested by life.

Working with a coach is a lot like having these old-souls in your life who can do for you what they did for me. They helped me to find my way and they believed in me when I wasn't so sure

Chapter 6: *Meet the Coach*

about myself. Their help over the years have been as priceless to me as working with a coach can be for you.

For instance, most of my life people have been drawn to me. They come up to me to share their stories or ask for my advice. I used to wonder why, until one of those wise old-souls told me that it was because I was a gifted listener.

My first reaction was disbelief.

To me, there wasn't anything special about listening. I thought everybody can listen, so I just didn't see why being a great listener was so valuable—until now.

While the road to figuring this out has been filled with twists and turns, it has been a rich journey that I probably would have never started if that wise old soul had not been in my life.

This is why, now that I'm a coach, I want to have the same lasting impact on people's lives that those old-souls had on mine.

Besides these old-souls, the other constant in my life has been that intuitive sense of knowing, my *north star*, that has guided me since I was that little girl who always knew there was a special place in the world just for her.

This intuition guided me to make a split second decision that led to my first highly rewarding career.

It has also given me the courage to take leaps of faith that have caused amazing things to happen for me throughout my life.

True, my life has certainly not been a piece of cake. Like everybody else, I've had hard times. But, I've had much more of those times when I've had to stop and say *wow!*—because, without realizing it, my intuition led me to where I had actually envisioned myself being years earlier.

These experiences have taught me that growth is not just a matter of going through hard times, but it is more a matter of taking a leap of faith, and mustering up the will to act intentionally to make things happen.

This is a lesson that I now try to pass on to my coaching clients.

I enjoy helping others take these leaps of faith in themselves, firm up their intentions, and find the will to do what it takes to reach their goals.

It's what I call, a *success consciousness*— the point where each person's intuition intersects with their individual intention and initiative, to produce successful results.

This process starts by helping clients to tune into what success means for them because this is the fuel that will drive them to muster up the will to succeed, in any area of life.

The next step is to help them honor that intuitive knowing inside of them since this will fuel their ability to act intentionally to get what they want.

I've used this process to help successful business and career women find the balance they need to perform at their peak at home, work, and in their businesses.

If you're one of these women, living an unbalanced life is probably causing you a lot of unnecessary stress that's robbing you of the joy and contentment you deserve for all your hard work.

But, you've probably put up with this unbalanced life because you believe it's just the price you have to pay for success—if you want it all.

Chapter 6: *Meet the Coach*

However, I want to give you permission to stop living your life by the myth that you can have it all. The uncomfortable truth is, you really *can't* have it all.

Life is about making choices; and, each choice comes with tradeoffs. You will never find the balance you want without letting go of something.

Knowing what to let go is the only way to really be successful at the right things, so your professional success does not come at the cost of the happy and satisfying personal life you want just as bad.

You probably already know this intuitively. But, unless you develop your own *success consciousness* it will be hard to find the clarity you need to stop living your life according to the expectations that others impose on you and start meeting your own expectations for your life.

If you can do this one thing, your outward success will not just be a façade that you're using to mask your misery. Instead, it will reflect the purpose that drives you from within, and it will free you up to be a peak performer in all areas of your life.

This is what it means to be successful at the right thing. And, it's the kind of success that I want for you.

That's why coaching is not just a job for me.

It's such an honor to be able to make a living by helping deserving people live the best version of themselves.

This is *my* definition of success; it is my *why,* or the purpose that drives me and that I intentionally pursue every day.

Accordingly, I see myself as the resource that the individuals I work with need to clarify, create, and then follow their own personal vision plan.

On the surface, this may seem simple to do.

But, as most coaches know, it's not easy for people to do the work they must do to conquer those self-imposed beliefs that stop them from moving forward, in their own best interests.

As a resource, I can provide the same kind of support that the old-souls were able to provide for me at pivotal points in my life.

I know how vulnerable it feels to have long-held beliefs challenged. That's why my coaching approach is anchored on a cornerstone of honesty and trust that gives me the moral authority needed to help my clients get the transformative breakthroughs they are looking for—and deserve.

Furthermore, since yoga has been such an important tool for me in helping me manage the stresses and fears in my own life and create deep personal connections with others, I consider it my secret weapon in my work with clients.

This is because it gives me the discipline to be centered and present in every interaction.

Being present allows me to give clients my undivided attention so I can listen with my complete heart and mind. Being centered is the art of ego control. It helps me to stay out of my clients' way so they can discover their own answers, instead of me trying to prove to them that I have all the answers.

These skills allow me to develop deep connections with those I work with because they sense that I don't want to control them. Knowing this is liberating for them because it reinforces their own efforts to let go of situations they can't control and frees them up to connect deeply with what matters most to them.

This is how I've been able to help so many of my clients achieve life-changing breakthroughs.

Here's how one of them describes her transformation:

> Dear Jen, what have you done for me? Lots.
>
> You listen to me and then you ask, *'why?'* What would my ideal life look like? You ask me to describe something I want to make a reality. Then you ask *'why?'* Why do I want this? What does it mean to *me?* The way you listen and talk to me, from the first time, really helped me focus on a detailed mission statement for my life. Not just a dream. A plan.
>
> You helped me see patterns in my life I never fully identified or appreciated.... You helped me change wishes into plans. You helped me divide things into steps so small I could take the first one. Your advice to, *'just do something'* and the positive reinforcement [I got] from achieving the first step ... leads to the next and next and eventually... done! The time chunking you showed me that helps me to get more done.... without feeling like I'm always starting from the beginning again. You've just done so much for me, Jen... Thank you. Thank you. Thank you.
>
> ~Laura, MD

My reply? Thank YOU!

I say, thank you to all my clients for allowing me to make the difference in this world that I always knew I was born to make.

About the Author. As a *Success & Life Balance Coach,* Jen Ryan specializes in working with ambitious career & professional women who want to balance their home and work life without having to be a superwoman or a saint. She helps them tap into their unique talents and succeed at the right things so they can reduce their stress, perform at their peak, and be more productive at home and work. She can be reached at JenRyanCoaching.com or **802-238-1897.**

Chapter 7

Final Thoughts

Jayne Logan & D. Forbes-Edelen

So, what now?

Now that you know what a Personal Coach is and isn't, and you know how to go about selecting one, what you can expect to pay, and what working with a coach can do for you, it's time to decide.

What transformation do YOU want?

Perhaps your life has taken a turn that you feel is wrong for you. Or, maybe you're tired of fighting with your boss, spouse, children, or workmates. Or, could it be that you're in a career or relationship that's stifling?

Or,

You may be running a business that has not been the success you dreamed. Or, you long to be a leader but can't convince people to follow you. Or, you may be feeling pressured because everyone else is running your life but you. Or, something else.

Whatever *it* is—if you are ready to make a change—do it!

But, don't do it alone.

If (as we intended), we've convinced you that you really can change your life, business, relationship, career, and just about anything else—with the help of your own personal coach—then find a Personal Coach today.

Chapter 7: Final Thoughts

And, if you're a coach, at whatever stage of your coaching development journey, we hope that this book can remind you of why you became a coach in the first place and of the value you have to offer.

Even more, we hope that it helps you to effectively communicate that value, and inspires you to remain committed to the high standards of excellence and professionalism that our profession demands—and that our clients deserve—if we are to have the positive impact on people's lives that motivated all of us to become coaches in the first place.

To continued transformations!

Looking for coaching resources for yourself or your clients?

We've put together a few for you, in the Appendix that follows. You will find the following resources:

Appendix A: *Selecting the Right Coach*

Appendix B: *Self-Coaching Tools*

- Goal Setting Worksheet
- Beat Procrastination
- Secrets to a GREAT LIFE
- Marketing Success Kit

Appendix C: *Coach Training Resources* for those interested in getting certified as Life, Health, or Clinical Health Coaches.

Enjoy...

◆ APPENDICES

List of Resources

Appendix A
Script for Selecting the Right Coach

Appendix B
Self-Coaching Tools for Personal & Business Life

- Goal Setting Worksheet
- Beat Procrastination
- Secrets to a GREAT LIFE
- Business Success Formula

Appendix C
Coach Training Resources for Certification in:

- Life Coaching
- Health Coaching
- Clinical Health Coaching

Appendix A

HOW TO SELECT THE RIGHT COACH

Script for Interviewing the Coach

Introduction:
I am interested in working with a Coach and I would like to ask a few questions about your practice.

Questions to ask:
1. Would you tell me a little bit about your coaching philosophy?
2. Why did you choose to become a coach?
3. Are you certified? By whom, or which company?
4. Do you have a formal Coaching Agreement?
5. Does your Agreement outline what I am responsible for, and what you commit to do?
6. Are your terms, confidentiality, and other policies included in the Agreement?
7. Do you have flexible hours?
8. How long could I expect our coaching sessions to last? (ex. 30 minutes, 1 hour, or something else?)
9. Have you had any clients you were unable to help accomplish what they set out to do?
10. What prevented that situation from being successful?

Summary/Close:
Thank you very much for your time. The information you have provided has been very helpful. I think we may be able to work together. I would like a little time to review the Coaching Agreement and will make a final decision in the next few days.

Appendix B

SELF COACHING TOOLS

Setting Goals

Goal Setting Worksheet
Jayne Logan | My Optimum Life

Goal (SMART objective):	
Benefit of achieving this goal:	
Target Completion Date:	Start Date:
What action steps are required in order to achieve the goal?	**Target Date**
1.	
2.	
3.	
4.	
5.	
Milestones Achieved	**Date Achieved**
1.	
2.	
3.	
Barriers to Success:	Strategy to Overcome Barriers:
Resources Required:	Notes

Source: Jayne Logan
© 2016. *My Optimum Life*. All Rights Reserved

APPENDICES: *Resources*

OVERCOMING PROCRASTINATION

Procrastination Bullies Worksheet | *Jen Ryan Coaching*
If you're struggling to achieve your goals, it's probably because you've got one of these bullies in your life bossing you around. Learn how to beat these bullies and finally get the success you want—and deserve.
Get it Here: *GetYourFreeGiftNow.com/fromJenRyan*

IMPROVING THE QUALITY OF EVERYDAY LIFE

The 9 Secrets | *Live a Great Life Coaching*
Get **9 Secrets to a Great Life** to learn the 9 essential (but surprisingly obvious) habits accomplished people practice every day to create a Great Life (and how you can make these your daily habits for better living too).
Get it Here: *GetYourFreeGiftNow.com/fromCynthia*

BUSINESS SUCCESS

The Marketing Success Formula | *by BiziWIFE*
If the toughest part of running your business is finding buyers and getting them to buy from *you*, then you need to know the ONE formula used by Disney, Sheraton, Smith Barney and other successful companies to find customers and keep them buying (and how to use it yourself—from an insider who knows). Getting clear on this one thing will take the mystery out of marketing and make it as easy as child's play for you to make money from your products, services, and ideas. Use this formula for business & marketing success and turn your marketing results from crappy to happy. **Get it Here:** *TheOneFormulaFor.MarketingYourBusinessWithoutSelling.com*

Appendix C

COACH TRAINING RESOURCES

Life Coaching Certification

International Coach Certification Alliance (ICCA)
Discover how to turn your love for helping others into a career as a Professional Life Coach.
http://FirstClassAuthors.com/RecommendsICCA

Health Coaching Certification

Institute for Integrative Nutrition (IIN)
If you have a passion for health & fitness this world renowned certification program will help you to turn that passion into a career helping others to develop healthy habits, get and stay in shape, and achieve lasting good health and wellness through good diet & nutrition choices.
http://FirstClassAuthors.com/RecommendsIIN

Clinical Health Coaching Certification

IOWA Chronic Care Consortium-Clinical Health Coach (CHC) Certification Program
Designed for Healthcare professionals and clinicians interested in making a larger impact in the care and management of chronic diseases by empowering patients and their caregivers.
http://FirstClassAuthors.com/RecommendsCHC

Made in the USA
Charleston, SC
29 February 2016